Crush Your Goals
The Ultimate Guide to Finishing Strong

Dr. Alberta Brown Green

Copyright © 2025 by Dr. Alberta Brown Green
All rights reserved.

No part of this publication may be reproduced, stored in a retrieval system, or transmitted in any form or by any means—electronic, mechanical, photocopying, recording, or otherwise—without the prior written permission of the author, except for brief quotations used in reviews, articles, or educational purposes.

The author is a licensed mental health professional. However, do not use this book in place of seeking mental or physical health advice. All content included in this book is for entertainment and inspirational purposes only.

Printed in the United States of America
First Edition

For more information about the author, to book an event, or obtain professional development for your organization, staff, or yourself, visit our website: www.abgpds.com

For permissions, inquiries, or additional resources, contact:
Dr. Alberta Brown Green
Email: mailto:info@abgpds.com

About the Author

Dr. Alberta Brown Green is a global leadership strategist, licensed mental health therapist, and award-winning CEO of ABG Professional Development Solutions. With over 25 years of experience, she has empowered thousands of professionals across industries through holistic leadership development, executive coaching, and organizational strategy.

Her dynamic career spans Fortune 500 consulting, higher academia, and workforce development, and her impact has earned her national recognition—including the Girl Scouts Women of Distinction Award and the Nashall "Shack" Harris Humanitarian Award.

Dr. Green holds a Ph.D. in Human Capital Development and is known as a strategic thought leader in the professional development world and is a renowned keynote speaker and facilitator. Her holistic signature approach helps leaders, organizations and individuals overcome perfectionism, procrastination, and fear of starting—replacing hesitation with clarity, confidence, and courageous action. She's a sought-after keynote speaker, board chair, and facilitator whose work transforms teams, organizations, and lives.

When she's not impacting and changing lives and facilitating workshops, or traveling for work, Alberta serves on multiple boards, supports military families, and enjoys music, theater, and tech gadgets.

She's been married to her best friend; the love of her life, Toby Green Sr., for 25 years and is the proud mom of two wonderful sons, Toby Jr. and Jacob Green.

Dedication

To the dreamers who have been told their goals are too big.
To the finishers who almost gave up but decided to try one more time.
To the ones sitting in silence, battling their own thoughts, wondering if they'll ever get it done—this is for you.
I dedicate these words to every person who has struggled with clarity, discipline, and the weight of unfinished business. May these pages remind you that you are not alone, that healing is part of the journey, and that you are fully capable of crossing the finish line.
And most of all, to my family and loved ones—thank you for being my anchor, my cheerleaders, and my constant reminder that every goal is worth pursuing when it's fueled by love, faith, and purpose.
With gratitude and fire,
Dr. Alberta Brown Green

Table of Contents

Crush Your Goals

INTRODUCTION 2

CHAPTER ONE: *NEW YEAR AND THE NEW YOU* 6

CHAPTER TWO: *SELF- REFLECT, ACKNOWLEDGE, AND ANALYZE YOUR PAST GOALS* 24

CHAPTER THREE: *CREATING NEW GOALS* 50

CHAPTER FOUR: *ADD STRATEGY TO YOUR GOALS* 67

CHAPTER FIVE: *MOTIVATE YOURSELF* 76

CHAPTER SIX: *COMMIT TO CONSISTENCY* 96

CHAPTER SEVEN: *CRUSH YOUR GOALS* 106

CHAPTER EIGHT: *FINDING YOUR WAY FORWARD: MENTAL WELLNESS AND THE POWER TO FINISH STRONG* 125

Introduction

It's no accident that this book found its way into your hands. Curiosity, frustration, hope, or even fate nudged you toward it. Maybe the cover caught your eye and whispered, "This could be the one that changes everything." So, you purchased it. And if you're like most of us, it's been sitting quietly on a shelf, collecting dust, waiting for you—while life kept moving, distractions piled up, and your goals stayed tucked in the background.

Maybe you've recently attended a life-changing training, conference, or workshop. You laughed, learned, and walked away with a notebook full of tools. As the days progressed, you slowly forgot about all that phenomenal, life-changing material—and then got swept right back into the whirlwind of everyday life. Perhaps you've always wanted to map out your life and career, but the "how" has felt overwhelming. Or you've been meaning to revisit your goal-setting skills, but the days keep slipping by. Or if we're being honest, you just need a jumpstart. A spark. A reason to shake off the slump that's been hanging around far too long.

You're tired of feeling behind. Tired of watching other people move forward while you're stuck in the same place. You're tired of waking up with good intentions, only to feel the weight of "too much" pushing you back into bed.

And then the questions creep in: What's wrong with me? Why do I feel so exhausted even though I haven't started my day? Why can't I just get up and do the things I said I would do?

Here's the truth: You're not a lazy bum. You're not hopeless. You're not a broken human. You may be caught in what I call **the fear of starting** — that quiet, sneaky belief that if you start, you won't finish. Over time, your brain starts to believe the story that you're someone who doesn't follow through.

That ends here.

***Crush Your* Goals** was written with YOU in mind—yes, you. This book is for individuals who are ready to get unstuck, pivot, and finally achieve the clarity, organization, and balance they have been craving. This book is also for your organization, boss, team, spouse, your best friend, your kids—anyone who's ready to live with more intention and crush their goals. Honestly, you could even use this book to set goals for your pet!

***Crush Your* Goals, *The Ultimate Guide to Finishing Strong*,** teaches you not only to set goals but to build a plan to CRUSH them—a family vision and goal-setting system that helped us not only dream big but actually achieve those dreams year after year. It taught us that visions and words have power, especially when they're written down and acted upon.

After 15 years of witnessing the transformation in my family, I shared the method with clients and friends, turning it into a life-changing workshop. And now, that same strategy of goal crushing is in your hands—my very first book!

This isn't a book to collect dust—it's a book to help you build victories. Read it. Use it. Work it. Let it change your life.

I can't wait to see what you accomplish—professionally, personally, and in every corner of your life—once you start crushing your goals.

Wishing you success in all that you do and love,

Dr. Alberta Brown Green

> EVERY DAY THAT YOU OPEN YOUR EYES IS AN OPPORTUNITY TO START FRESH...
>
> — DR. ALBERTA BROWN GREEN

Chapter One

New Year and the New You!

> *"Sometimes, starting is the hardest thing to do. However, once you start, commit to finish strong."*
>
> – Dr. ABG

Happy New Year and Happy New You! If you are reading this book and it's not the first month of the new year, it's okay—this work can be activated at any moment, and your season to start crushing goals can begin right now! This book is also designed to meet you exactly where you are and give you clear, energizing steps to turn intention into action! The New Year and the New YOU can begin anytime you choose—even today.

THANK YOU for choosing YOU and for stepping into a path of purpose and progress. THANK YOU for deciding to do better, be better, and live better by investing in YOU. Get ready to enhance and sharpen your focus, learn simple habits that build momentum, and consistency tools to keep you moving forward even during challenging times.

Are you ready to commit to crushing your goals?

Understandably, some people feel overwhelmed with the concept of planning and goal-setting because of their fear of commitment. That fear can make the process feel heavy and nearly impossible. Others desire to be more organized and goal-oriented but wish it would magically happen. My client, who had decided to take planning for the future seriously, shared that when her friends, family, or work buddies mention planning or organization, she hears, "Let's plan out the whole, long, anything-can-happen year of the unknown so that you can be tied down to this one plan, and you are a loser if you don't accomplish everything that you said you would accomplish." You might perceive her statement as overly dramatic, or you might think, "Wow—that lady is reading my mind."

No matter your thoughts, I want you to know that commitment here is not a rigid vow but a promise to yourself. I assure you that if you commit to incorporating this book into your personal and professional life, you will effortlessly achieve your resolutions, goals, and plans—in other words, crush your goals!

Before you read any further, please sign your name to confirm that you are committed to crushing your goals.

Name: _____ Date: _____

Thank you for your signature of commitment! Let's review why millions of people set resolutions, create goals, or seek meaningful change in their work and life.

Millions of people make resolutions

As strange as it may sound, not just a few hundred, but millions of people make New Year resolutions every single year. That's crazy, huh? Most people write down a few resolutions, either in December or January, of how they will change their lives forever. The famous "I'm going to leave my job, drop 20 to 40 pounds, run a 5k, or clean out my closet" are a few of my favorites. When resolutions are made, people truly have honest intentions to accomplish them or make them happen. However, Life Be-Life-En …. in other words, you may be unable to complete your resolution due to unforeseen circumstances. For instance, **YOU NEED A NEW JOB.** Everything at work is burning down all around you. You absolutely hate it there. You are not growing, your boss is mean, and you don't feel like you belong. Not to mention, every time you look up, someone is being fired or let go. To make matters worse, you realize that it is time for you to politely bow out (quit), but you hesitate to do so because you need your paycheck. You continue to arrive, following the same routine of crying, praying, and swallowing two extra-strength Tylenol with a mouthful of water before drying your eyes and exiting the car to walk into the building of dread.

Better yet, **YOU NEED TO LOSE WEIGHT**. You had very good intentions to drop 20 pounds before the new year because your doctor said you have signs of a fatty liver and you are approaching pre-diabetes. You decided, no matter what, you would shed at least 20 pounds and do your best to stay away from sugary treats and fatty foods. However, while you were making these declarations in your mind, you had no idea that the love of your life would break your heart. Now, ice cream, sweets, and depression have become your new best friends.

Your new group of friends provides a sense of comfort that you know isn't right, yet you welcome good old chocolate chip ice cream, soft, fluffy birthday cake (and it's not your birthday), and woe-is-me depression to the party.

Maybe **YOU NEED TO BE MORE FIT**. So, you're not in the "drop a few pounds" resolution category, but you decided on the health journey kick, including completing "the mighty 5-k" attempt! You decided to be fitter because someone told you that it would help with your physical health and mood. Not to mention, your doctor told you that you had hypertension (high blood pressure). You were so pumped! You purchased new workout gear, with new matching tennis shoes, and said to yourself, "Forget the couch to 5k; I'm jumping in headfirst, baby! Who needs to stretch and prep?"

So, you wake up, put on your shorts, don't stretch, and just start running like a mad person because your mind told you, "These old bones were something back in the day!" And what usually happens is that you burn yourself out in the first few days and meet up with your friends, ice cream, sweets, and depression.

Career resolutions and goals

Individuals who are currently employed place a high level of importance on career advancement opportunities, including raises, promotions, growth, and development opportunities at entry-level, intermediate, junior, and senior-level roles. In today's rocket-speed, ever-changing workplace, people are expected to do more with less on a daily basis. Employees are expected to invest in continued on-and-off-the-job learning, training, and development—even at their expense.

Workers are practically drinking from a firehose (a reactive work environment), and it is not only expected but required. Some people experience working for organizations that are struggling to make ends meet and constantly laying people off. Other people work for companies that are growing and acquiring other companies so fast that there is no stability in job security—meaning when the acquisitions and mergers happen, individuals, teams, and full departments will be terminated.

This phenomenon is why you or some of your friends are constantly looking for a new job. At the beginning of the year, most people have three to five career resolutions or career goals that usually outnumber and outrank other resolutions on their lists.

There are several reasons people create resolutions regarding their professional careers. **Loss of interest** in their role or the company they work for is a common one. When bored or unfulfilled on the job, a person may find themselves constantly watching the clock. One hour of work, for example, could feel like an eight-hour shift! Imagine waking up day after day and doing the exact same thing, like you are on autopilot—you are unchallenged and unfulfilled. For instance, nothing about the job is exciting anymore, but you are trying your absolute best to stay motivated and complete your tasks.

Unbeknownst to you, everyone thinks you're lazy, taking up space, and just there to collect a paycheck. Truth be told.....yes, you are bored out of your mind, and yes, you may call in sick several times a month, but you are doing your best to stay present. You know you should leave, but you need the money because you have this little responsibility called "bills," so you stay at your place of employment... day after day with limited motivation, not living up to your full potential, doing the bare minimum to get by.

Companies offering merit increases, career mobility **opportunities (promotions)**, and professional development are other reasons people create resolutions regarding staying or leaving their place of employment. For instance, if you haven't received a merit increase (raise) in three years due to budget cuts, that could signal concerns for career growth and opportunities.

Moreover, if you have consistently performed excellently by arriving at work on time, maintaining a positive attitude, meeting and exceeding your work goals, and proactively learning and contributing over the past three years without ever being promoted to the next level, it may lead to concerns about your career advancement.

When it comes to **professional development**, some organizations believe in investing in their employees by sending them to training to enhance their skills as employees and individuals. Furthermore, the company may encourage continued education credits in their career field. However, there are companies that don't have professional development budgets and will not support paying for employees or company-wide professional development. If your employer meets one or two of your needs, you may consider staying. And of course, if your employer is not meeting either of those needs, you may consider leaving.

Lastly, escape from a **hostile work environment** falls on the list of career resolutions and goals. First, let's describe a 'hostile work environment.' A hostile work environment is a workplace that makes employees feel "insecure, uncomfortable, fearful, or intimidated" due to unwelcome actions from their supervisors and/or co-worker(s). These actions may include verbal abuse, discrimination, unwanted touching, overworking individuals without pay, and constant disrespect or belittling.

You may be in a hostile work environment if you feel like you're back on the playground, enduring bullying. The trouble with a hostile work environment is that some people feel they can't speak up or leave due to fear of retaliation or losing their job, which could lead to financial difficulties.

Financial resolutions and goals

Finances significantly impact both work and life. Forbes Health conducted a survey revealing that improving finances was one of 2024's top New Year resolutions. For most, good financial resolutions are being able to care for your or your family's needs and some of their wants, not living paycheck to paycheck, access to an emergency fund, and a decent savings account. For some, it's having a decent credit score, the ability to budget for your needs and a few wants, and ownership of an IRA or 401k. For others, financial health is being debt-free, owning properties and land, having the ability to make money while sleeping, and establishing generational wealth. Which category relates to you?

Failure to establish financial resolutions or goals can lead to stress and anxiety. Troubled finances, at all different levels, interrupt a person's career, lifestyle, and well-being. Believe it or not, financial challenges often lead to feelings of hopelessness and anxiety, significantly impacting your mental and physical health, relationships, and overall quality of life. I am assuming that is the reason improving finances comfortably ranks among the top resolutions every year.

During the 2020 pandemic, an American Psychological Association (APA) study found that 72% of Americans felt stressed about money. Throughout the pandemic, companies were hemorrhaging from losing customers and business. Therefore, some companies were unable to pay their employees, which led to massive layoffs. Workers were worried they couldn't feed their families or pay bills due to furloughs or layoffs.

Financial challenges can lead to relationship problems and broken marriages. Marriages and relationships are challenging enough, but if you throw money in the mix—watch out!

For instance, one of the most common reasons for divorce in 2024 was financial issues that caused a tremendous strain on marriages of both low and high earners (https://www.wf-lawyers.com/).

In marriages and committed relationships, when there is a lack of or no communication about money, it ultimately becomes a lack of trust. In relationships, when there is a lack of communication concerning financial goals, hiding spending habits and not letting each other know about major purchases can lead to ignoring the true magnitude of the accumulated amount of debt. In turn, such silence can lead to arguing, feeling hopeless, and having resentment in the relationship. Mismanagement of funds can also lead to eviction from your home. Lastly, financial problems can cause physical and mental well-being issues that can ultimately lead to stress, anxiety, and depression.

Fitness health resolutions and goals

Did you know that the number one resolution for 2024 was to improve fitness? According to Cincinnati (WKRC), Forbes Health conducted a new survey revealing that improved fitness levels were the top New Year resolution (48%), followed by improving mental health (36%) and losing weight (33.8%). Interesting how fitness, finances, and mental health are sitting pretty and cozy together—huh?

Regarding fitness resolutions, some may include enrolling in an exercise class, joining a gym, building muscle, finding a few 15-minute workout videos that work for you, or walking. It is easy to understand why so many people create resolutions around improving their fitness levels due to the many benefits that can happen to the body. Exercising regularly can help manage or even prevent health issues or challenges such as heart attacks, strokes, type 2 diabetes, high blood pressure, being overweight, and osteoporosis. Something as simple as walking, biking, cardio, weightlifting, and jogging can help combat health conditions, diseases, and weight gain.

Regarding weight gain, how often have you asked yourself, "Why am I so fat? Why do I have no energy? Why am I so stiff?" "Where did this heartburn come from? When and how did this happen?" All of these thoughts travel through your mind at the speed of light, all while you are lying on the couch, eating Doritos (the big bag), finishing your third chocolate chip cookie, and washing it down with a Diet Coke. Of course, you think, "If I could only drop about X pounds, I would feel and look a lot better. The reason you think you would feel better if you became more fit is that it's a true thought. When your body functions at its optimal fitness and weight for your frame, height, and age, you feel better, look better, and have more energy compared to when you are overweight.

Everyone benefits from physical activity, no matter your ability, sex, or age. Exercise increases not only your energy level but also your mood, feeds your muscles oxygen, and increases blood flow throughout the circulatory system, which will keep your organs functioning and working properly.

When you exercise, you burn calories, and the more calories you burn, the more fat you burn. Not only do you burn fat from working out, but your body also releases harmful toxins from your digestive system, liver, kidneys, skin, and lungs through your sweat glands. Exercise is even beneficial for your brain health!

Mental health resolutions and goals

As mentioned earlier in Forbes Health, improving mental health made up 36% of New Year's resolutions for 2024. The pandemic, the relentless exposure of social media, and broader national stressors have contributed to a noticeable rise in people wanting to take care of their mental health. For instance, COVID disrupted our daily routines and amplified isolation and uncertainty, causing self-care and emotional wellbeing to become staples in goal-setting. As of today, mental health resolutions and goals have become mainstream and less taboo in the workplace. The normalization of mental health has led to leaders and colleagues being more supportive of creating space to support necessary work adjustments due to mental health and wellbeing needs.

Good mental health is when you can regulate your emotions and moods in a positive way. You are content and discover joy, happiness, and fulfillment in the emotional, physical, and spiritual aspects of life. Other attributes of good mental health are having decent sleep patterns, positive thoughts and outlets, and you can easily bounce back from challenging situations. Moreover, having low-stress levels and your finances under control.

Lastly, good mental health has a limited amount of negative thoughts, self-sabotage, anxiety, depression, low mood, and anger. Overall, mental health resolutions involve anything that will improve your mood, attitude, and mental state.

Below is a list of mental health resolutions and goals.
- Lowering your stress level
- Setting boundaries
- Becoming more assertive
- Being kind to yourself
- Giving yourself and others grace
- Listening more to your body's needs
- Forgiving yourself for past mistakes
- Enrolling in therapy
- Allowing yourself to have downtime
- Limiting screen time

Have you had any challenges with any of the mental health resolutions and goals mentioned earlier? If so, which ones? Have you ever received mental health counseling? If so or if not, what are your thoughts about it?

Reflections:

A minimum of 9% of Americans follow through on their goals and resolutions.

With millions of people creating resolutions leading up to the new year and beyond, research indicates that only 9% of Americans follow through on their resolutions. Knowing that only 9% of people keep their resolutions should help you give yourself grace. As a **career** and executive coach who utilizes a holistic approach to career development, I meet several people from all walks of life who declare several of the goals and resolutions mentioned previously. Some are seeking advancement or a promotion at their current place of business, a new position at a different company, or a brand-new career—something they've always wanted to do in life.

Others are seeking guidance and tools to communicate more effectively with their supervisor, boss, and/or co-workers. Others need help navigating and learning how to survive in a hostile work environment. Some are exhausted, overworked, and burned out. Some have made it to the final destination in their career and are seeking a smooth transition into retirement.

However, as a subject matter expert in career exploration and goal setting, I've helped several people explore different career options, create career goals, and follow through with their goals, plans, and aspirations.

The information in the following chapters is the same guidance I have used for nearly 15 years to help clients do better, be better, and become better. These are proven practices drawn from coaching sessions, leadership workshops, and real-world outcomes that consistently move people from stuck to forward motion. Read these pages with the confidence that these tools were developed and utilized by real people.

As you navigate this book, you will encounter practical and clear tips to help you set sound goals and build strategies for your life and career. Some of the chapters include focused exercises designed to move you from idea to action, plus short, repeatable frameworks you can use in meetings, planning sessions, or daily routines. The intent is simple: make goal-setting less complicated and more reliably effective.

You will also find writing prompts and reflection sections that invite you to answer questions, capture insights, and record moments of clarity. Use these prompts to clarify priorities, surface patterns, and commit to the next right step.

At the end of the day, everyone wants the same thing: progression, a sense of accomplishment, and the ability to keep moving forward. Happiness and confidence grow when you feel aligned with your choices and can see progress measured in both small wins and larger milestones. This book focuses on sustainable, constant progress rather than quick fixes.

This book is structured so that each chapter builds on the last. Expect to revisit sections as you grow, recalibrate when needed, and celebrate milestones along the way. Commit to practicing the exercises, tracking your attempts, and letting the momentum of small wins carry you to the bolder goals you truly want!

What's one goal that keeps you up at night that this book may help you accomplish?

Reflections:

> **HONEST REFLECTION REQUIRES CONFRONTING GOALS LEFT UNFINISHED.**
>
> — DR. ALBERTA BROWN GREEN

Chapter Two

Self-Reflect, Acknowledge, and Analyze Your Past Goals

"Owning what you didn't finish is the first step to self-reflection; giving yourself grace is next."
– Dr. ABG

Self-reflect on your past goals

Self-reflection on past goals is a priceless act of kindness toward yourself; it invites you to step back and mentally review what actually happened, celebrate progress, and honor the effort you invested, even when outcomes fell short. I encourage you to look back with curiosity rather than judgment. Ask clear questions—Why did I give up on this goal? Why did certain deadlines slip? Which goals caused stress and why? Self-reflection helps you notice patterns without shaming yourself and builds confidence for what comes next. Pay close attention to the values, emotions, and motivations that guided those goals and how they shifted over time. Notice the behaviors and triggers that preceded setbacks and the conditions that supported success. Recognize when fatigue, perfectionism, or competing priorities influenced your choices and identify the one remarkable goal you achieved to understand what worked.

These insights reveal where you are now and show practical pivots you can make to protect your energy and align future efforts with what truly matters.

Lastly, use what you learn to redesign goals that respect your rhythms, strengths, and limits. Convert reflections into specific adjustments: simplify a step, build in rest, and ask for support. Be willing to reframe timelines or remove goals that no longer serve you. Treat your reflection time as a deliberate, generous practice that clarifies which goals to keep, which to release, and how to move forward with intention. This kind, informed approach turns past experience into a sustainable plan for growth and honors the person you are becoming!

Limit all distractions

Now that you have a better understanding of self-reflection and why it matters, let's dive in! Before you begin your reflection, **limit all distractions**—this is a must. A distraction is anything that pulls your attention away from what you're doing. It can take many forms—like your smartphone, the TV, other people, or even unrelated tasks on your to-do list.

Smart phones can be a distraction

Smartphones can be a pesky distraction when trying to get things done. Two terms to describe smartphone overuse are "smartphone addiction" and "smartphone dependence."

For some people, the phone is the first thing they grab to share good or bad news. When feelings of sadness or boredom arise, they reach for their phone. In a world of constant connectivity, most people's smartphones are with them 24/7.

Occasionally, it seems as if people are in an emotional relationship with their phones. For example, they grab their phone before getting out of bed. Better yet, smartphones are taken into private places, like the bathroom. People brush their teeth or even use the toilet, all while scrolling on their smartphones. Some even place their phone in the shower or by the tub when bathing. Finally, some individuals bring their phones to bed with them, and the device rests on its own pillow! The only thing the phone is missing is a soft blanket to keep it warm!

You would think that people separate from their phones while they are sleeping. However, research shows that some people need their phone to sleep. They may scroll until they fall asleep or have their earbuds in, listening to music, videos, etc., while sleeping.

Recommendation for smartphone distraction

Let's face it, social media of any kind can rob you of minutes or hours of your day. I recommend turning it off or on airplane mode before starting your self-reflection. If you try to self-reflect without turning off your cell phone, you may be tempted to text, scroll through TikTok, Facebook, Instagram, or X formally known as Twitter. If this is challenging to you, create a simple boundary of leaving your phone in another room with the ringer turned off. Set a 10-minute timer, during your reflection time to check your social media, texts, and any missed phone calls.

Television can be a distraction

The television could be a distraction as well. You may think TVs are less distracting than smartphones, but today's smart TVs are basically large smartphones with all the same features. Televisions have the ability to perform recording, pausing, and fast-forwarding through commercials and scenes, which makes it so easy to binge-watch your favorite series or new movie releases. Television is definitely a distraction if you enjoy watching news, sports, or reality TV. And of course, since most televisions are now SMART TVs, you have endless streaming options making it easy to lose track of time because trust me... there is a channel app just for you, with all of your favorite shows, waiting to take you down a three-hour rabbit hole of TV watching.

Recommendation for television distraction

Reflect with the TV OFF. If this is challenging, create simple boundaries like a two-episode rule, a timer, or a fixed "screen-off" hour to protect your focus and energy time.

You can treat TV as a planned break or reward rather than an escape plan. Use it as a buffer to refresh you without derailing the progress you're making toward your reflection process.

People can be a distraction

Do your best to avoid conversations during your reflection time, whether they involve talking on the phone with energy-draining individuals or conversing with those who bring you joy. For instance, after finally mustering the energy to gather and sort two weeks' worth of dirty clothes from around the house, your phone rings. It's your sister who you enjoy talking about EVERYTHING with. But you tell yourself, "I can talk to her and multitask!" However, three hours later (the time you allotted for laundry day), you are still on the phone, but now, you are sitting on the recliner, talking, laughing, and finishing up the Netflix series both of you were binge-watching together last week.

OR the phone rings, and it is your friend who is going through a rough patch, and every time you talk with them, the sky is falling, and everything that could possibly go wrong in their life is happening. You tell yourself, "Ok… just 15 minutes and I will get back at it." But no. They are talking a mile a minute, all while sobbing and crying.

Recommendation for people distraction

I recommend informing individuals who may need

you, that you will be unreachable during the hours of x and x. I understand that some of you may have children, elderly parents, or friends that have unlimited access to you. Therefore, treat your reflection time like a doctor's appointment or a massage. Most people are unreachable during those types of appointments.

Tasks can be a distraction

Lastly, tasks, even important tasks, can derail your reflection time. For instance, you have finally decided to carve out time to reflect on your past goals. You have pen and paper in hand but suddenly every other unfinished task starts fighting for your attention. Things you need to get done, such as cleaning the kitchen, going to the dentist, dropping clothes off at the cleaners, following up with your boss or team on projects, putting gas in your car, assisting your kid(s) with school/work assignments, and spending dedicated quality time with a significant other, can always get in the way of fulfilling your commitments. Your busy, stressful, and amazing life sprinkled with procrastination makes it hard for you to be great and do what you said you would do.

Recommendation for task distraction

Stop your tasks from becoming a distraction by writing down three important tasks you need to complete by a certain time today, and two unimportant ones. Put the list to the side and once you finish reflecting, you can work on your list.

What are some obstacles that constantly get in the way of you completing or fulfilling your commitments?

Reflections:

Choosing your reflection time and location

Choosing a time to reflect or work on a goal starts with choosing the best time that works for your internal clock. Our internal clock helps us figure out when we are more productive. Did you know birds have internal clocks? Some are early birds, and others are night owls.

Let's say you had a choice of two birds; which would you be? An early bird, such as the American Robin or a night owl, such as the Northern Spotted Owl?

An early bird, such as the American Robin, is the first bird that gets the worm—literally. It rises early and provides the first beautiful melody or song we hear in the spring and summer, often before the break of dawn. Their agility, energy, and love of the sun make them excellent creators.

If your internal clock lines up with the American Robin (early bird), you tend to naturally rise early, and you are more productive in the morning. The morning time is when you do your best thinking and are the happiest.

A night owl, such as the Northern Spotted Owl, owns the night! Owls are nocturnal birds, sleep during the day, and live at night. Their large size, wide body, and sharp claws make them excellent hunters. They sleep all through the day and wake up around dusk, and their eyes shine through the night like flashlights. When they are finished flying, hunting, and watching, they head back home to their nesting place.

When the sun starts to rise, they are just closing their eyes. If your internal clock lines up with the Northern Spotted Owl (night owl), you tend to be more productive at night, which enhances your thinking and increases your activity levels.

Determining your reflection time

To determine your preferred time for reflection, experiment with working on important tasks or projects during different times of the day. Also, pay attention to when you have the most amount of free time, the clearest thinking and most reliable energy. Do this for at least one week. At the end of the week, you should have a good idea of your internal clock system – meaning if you work better in the morning or better at night.

After you've observed yourself for a week, come back to this page and write down your preferred reflection time.

*Reflections:*_____

_____

_____

_____

_____

_____

Now that you've decided what time of the day works best for you, choose an activity or goal you want to pursue during this time, and try it out. For instance, let's say you made up your mind last week that you would start your exercise workout plan on Monday at 6:00 am (because you discovered you are a morning person). Sunday night, you go to bed telling yourself that you will wake up a few minutes early to get dressed and exercise. You are so excited and anxious to keep your commitment to exercising that you wake up a few times through the night, checking the clock, to make sure you don't oversleep. Now it is 3:45 am, two hours and 15 minutes before your scheduled workout time, and you can't sleep. So, you grab your phone, play around on social media, and the next thing you know, you are finally sleepy and it is 6:05 am. At that moment, you decide to roll over and sleep until 7:30 am because you have to be at work at 8:30 am. You tell yourself, "Wow – how did this happen?"

I will be the first to tell you that things happen, and habits take time to stick. Just because you weren't able to keep your commitment doesn't mean that mornings don't work for you. It means that tomorrow is a new day, and you can try again. After a week has gone by, and you are still hitting the snooze button, sleeping through your alarm, or barely able to slip on your workout gear, maybe consider exercising in the evening.

Location for reflection time

Location is key during your reflection time. I suggest choosing a location for your reflection time that is free from distractions. Your home may not be the best place to reflect. There may be temptations floating around, such as surfing the television, talking on the phone, finishing up a few baskets of laundry, or ANYTHING besides reflecting on your past goals.

Recommendation for reflection time

I recommend leaving your home. If you leave your home, consider the local library. It's usually quiet, not a lot of noise, and you may not know many people there who will try and talk to you. Better yet, try a coffee shop. You can load up on the caffeine and get your mind going in a relaxing atmosphere.

Maybe consider nature—a local park. Nice breezes flowing over you while sitting at a park bench under a shade tree sounds calming and relaxing. Nature may be just what you need to open up your mind for reflection.

If you absolutely cannot leave your home, consider choosing a space that you don't typically use, such as the basement, the kitchen table, or your closet. I actually transformed my closet, complete with clothes inside, into a secret space dedicated to writing, meditation and reflection. If your closet is not big enough, consider any room in your house that you don't spend a lot of time in.

Either way, the best time to reflect is when you are more intentional and have a clear mind for thinking. As a reminder, when reflecting on your past goals, choose a time that works for you and a location away from the radio, social media, the news, unneeded conversations, and phone calls before doing the work.

Before you start your process, close your eyes and take a few deep breaths. Breathe in through your nose and out through your mouth to relieve any stress or anxiety about this process. Let's get to work, acknowledge your past goals (resolutions), and acknowledge why you did not complete them. What are your thoughts on reflection?

*Reflections:*_____

_____
_____
_____
_____
_____
_____
_____
_____
_____
_____
_____
_____

Goals, goals, goals

Every single person on Earth has either set goals for themselves or hoped to achieve them. Setting goals is fun for some people, but difficult for others. A goal or resolution is an idea of what you want to accomplish in the future. Another definition of a goal is an outcome that an individual or organization aspires to attain.

Now that you've eliminated all distractions, determined a decent time and location to reflect on your goals, and completed a few breathing techniques to lower stress, let's get to work. Grab a notebook and your favorite pen. Sometimes, it's good to go old-school when reflecting—meaning pen and paper. If you absolutely hate writing, go ahead and grab your laptop, but be mindful not to become distracted by emails and notification pings.

Furthermore, watch out for the temptation to check your social media accounts or the route of your five Amazon packages.

Ok, back to business. Take a moment to explore and answer the questions below.

1. What goals did you create?
2. What goals did you accomplish and not accomplish?
3. If you did not complete your goals, what obstacles prevented you from doing so?
4. Were the goals you created realistic and attainable?

What goals did you create?

Usually, goals or resolutions are created close to the end of the year or right before the beginning of the year. People often set different types of goals to enhance various aspects of their lives. Some common goals fall within health and fitness, professional and personal development, career/work, education, and financial goals. Oh, and we can't forget relationships and social, mental, and emotional goals.

When reflecting on your goals, jot down every single one of them. I am sure several of your goals landed in the categories mentioned in the previous chapter. Now, pull out that favorite pen of yours and take a moment to write out your past goals.

What goals did you accomplish or not accomplish?
*Reflections:*_____

_____
_____
_____
_____
_____
_____
_____
_____
_____

Now that you have your list of goals in front of you, please read through them. Next, take your pen and place a "checkmark" beside every goal that you accomplished and an "x" beside every goal that you did not accomplish. Take another sheet of paper and fold it in half, vertically. In the top left corner of the page, title it "Goals I Accomplished," and in the top right corner of the page, title it "Goals Not Accomplished." Next, use the list of goals you made in the last exercise, where you marked which ones were completed with checkmarks and which ones were not with x's. Put the completed goals on the left and the uncompleted goals on the right side of the paper. Please take a moment to reflect on what you have accomplished and what was not accomplished.

What are your thoughts about what you wrote?
*Reflections:*_____

_____
_____
_____
_____
_____
_____
_____
_____

Analyzing past goals: Four-block exercise

Now that you have a list of completed and uncompleted goals, it's time to analyze your goals. One of my favorite songs is by a group called "En Vogue." The song has a verse that says, "Free your mind, and the rest will follow." I love that verse because sometimes, we have to move away from all distractions to properly free our minds enough to think deeply. Analysis, for the most part, requires deep thinking. Take a moment to grab a sheet of paper and of course, your favorite pen.

Let's try the Four Block Exercise to analyze your goals.

First, fold your paper in half vertically, open it back up, and fold it once again, horizontally. There should be four squares. In the top left square, title it "what went well during the past six months." In the top right square, title it "What went wrong during the past six months." In the bottom left square, title it "what you learned," and in the bottom right square, title it "what you will do next."

See below:

Top Left Square—what went well in the past six months

Top Right Square—What Went Wrong in the past six months

Bottom Left Square—What did you learn in the past six months?

Bottom Right Square—What will you do in the next six months?

Before you start answering the title questions in each box, I would like to share a tidbit of information about the purpose of the exercise. This exercise is to review your goals for the past six months of the year. Technically, you can chart a year's worth of goals as well; however, I recommend six months so that you don't become overwhelmed.

Back to the exercise. Look at your list of goals. What have you achieved in the last six months, and what good experiences have you encountered? Write that information down in the top left square.

Examples of goals and life's wins someone may place in this box are listed below:

1. I purchased a new car
2. I enrolled in college
3. I received a promotion at work
4. I became certified in my profession
5. I was a bridesmaid/groomsman in my best friend's wedding
6. I lost 20 pounds
7. I have a new boyfriend/girlfriend
8. I joined a nice church
9. I started a new business
10. My blood pressure is now under control
11. I finally purchased my first home
12. I managed to save 1,000 for my emergency fund

In the top right square, write down the goals you didn't achieve and what was going on in your life that may have caused you not to complete the goals.

Examples of goals and life challenges someone may place in this box are listed below:

1. I was not able to purchase a new car because I did not save up enough money

2. I had to sit out a semester of school because of my grades

3. I did not receive the promotion I so desperately needed because I wasn't qualified

4. I was diagnosed with high blood pressure

5. I gained 30 pounds due to stress

6. I don't like getting out much, and I don't like people

7. My boyfriend/girlfriend broke up with me because they thought I wasn't doing anything with my life

8. I had a major loss/death in my family that has caused me to become depressed

9. I had to move out of my house because I couldn't afford the mortgage

10. I was diagnosed with an autoimmune disease, and I am very tired all the time

In the bottom left square, write out the key lessons you learned about yourself in the past six months.

Examples of key learnings someone may place in this box are listed below:

1. The reason I couldn't afford a new car is that I mismanaged my money, and my credit was not the best
2. I couldn't concentrate in school due to relationship issues, which caused my grades to be bad and led me to drop out for a semester.
3. I had no idea my boyfriend/girlfriend desired to leave me because I was too busy dealing with my own problems
4. I was told I didn't get the promotion due to a company merger and that the person from the other company was more qualified
5. I don't think I have many true friends because I don't know how to engage with people or show that I am friendly
6. I gained 20 pounds this past six weeks because, honestly, I am not happy, and I haven't figured out how to deal with all of the stressors I encounter daily
7. I lost my house because I had a major illness that kept me out of work for several months
8. My grades suffered because I did not study enough

Lastly, in the bottom right square, write out what you plan to do or would like to do in the next six months.

Examples of plans someone may place in this box are listed below:

1. Pay off a specific debt (e.g., credit cards, student loans, money you owe people)

2. Reduce relationship and work stress by setting clear boundaries

3. Commit to creative hobbies like painting, reading, or photography

4. Set a diet plan and prepare a week's worth of meals every Sunday to maintain healthy eating habits

5. Perform a true job search and go on at least two interviews

6. Join a church, meet new people, and be more friendly

7. Commit to getting healthy by exercising up to three times a week.

8. Plan my first trip out of the country

9. Start a business or take my business to the next level

10. Start actively dating

11. Find a mentor in my field of education or business

12. Start saving for an emergency fund account

Reviewing your goals consists of reflecting on your achievements, challenges, and learnings. This reflection will give you insight into what worked for you, and what didn't. Also, the Four-block Exercise helps you identify gaps, which sheds light on what went right and what went wrong during the past six months. Furthermore, you can determine where you fell short on your goals and understand why and how it happened.

Alright. Now that you have your goals and the Four Block Exercise detailing your goals before you, please take a moment to analyze them. Notice how many you've accomplished—awesome job! Pat yourself on the back! Now, notice how many of your goals you did not accomplish. Give yourself grace.

Overall, were the goals you created realistic or unrealistic?
*Reflections:*_____
_____
_____
_____
_____
_____
_____
_____

Realistic goals are those you can achieve with your current resources, skills, and time. An example of a realistic goal is waking up in the morning and brushing your teeth—ha! Ok, ok, ok…. I was just trying to make you laugh. But seriously, that is a realistic goal. Did you know that some people wake up late, rush around searching for something to wear to work, and don't have time to brush their teeth, eat breakfast, or even use the bathroom out of fear of being terribly late? Yes, it happens.

Another realistic goal may be to save $250.00 in three months by not eating out or spending money on things that are not necessary, like fast food, DoorDash, or something that caught your eye at 1:00 am while browsing Amazon.

Are your goals unrealistic? Typically, unrealistic goals are overly ambitious and beyond your current resources, time, or skills. Occasionally, when we create goals, we shoot for the moon, and we are hopeful to land among the stars. However, with an unrealistic goal, instead of shooting for the moon, one may shoot for planet Jupiter. When you have big goals and no resources or the slightest idea of how to complete them, they may be unrealistic. An example of an unrealistic goal is believing you can become a social media influencer millionaire in six months without any specific training, resources, business knowledge about the craft, or any skin in the game. I'm not saying it's impossible…. Just unrealistic.

Unrealistic goals often lead to frustration, stress, and a loss of motivation because they lack clarity and structure. These goals are usually vague, making it hard to define what success looks like or how to measure progress. Also, goals that are unrealistic lack clear completion timeframes and may not align with your values or long-term goals.

Whether your goals are realistic or unrealistic, they are yours. Let's review which of your goals have been achieved.

*Reflections:*_____

_____
_____
_____
_____
_____
_____
_____

Give yourself grace

You are not alone in feeling overwhelmed by unfinished tasks, goals, hopes, and dreams that seem nearly impossible to accomplish. It is common for the majority of people to attempt to improve themselves during the first few months of the year. Nevertheless, such tasks can be difficult to accomplish because individuals are simply attempting to keep up with the pace of life during that time.

It's also common for people to have a fantastic start to the year but then fizzle out around the middle of January. Trust me, as the young folks say, "life be lifing." That statement means that it appears that everything is falling apart all around you. For instance, you may feel as if you can't get ahead, whether it's at work, school, in relationships, or with finances. This can cause a person to feel all alone in their journey. It is normal to be hard on yourself sometimes, but remember what I shared earlier - give yourself grace.

Giving yourself grace means realizing that you are not alone in the world of unfinished goals, tasks, or resolutions. Millions of people are pursuing their goals, equipped with vision boards worthy of a Pinterest Hall of Fame. But when it's time to execute, the drive disappears and nothing moves forward. Between December 1 and January 31, more goals are abandoned than gym memberships. Time passes, obstacles arise, and the goal fails to reach its completion. However, be encouraged and don't give up. Be kind to yourself. Personally, regarding gearing up for the new year, I practice being kind to myself by beginning my new year on February 1.

Lastly, not even the world was created in a day. Biblically speaking, it took six days to create the world, and even God the Father gave himself grace and rested on the seventh day.

Take a moment to write down a few times in your life when you showed grace to a friend, a family member, or yourself.

Reflection:_____

_____
_____
_____
_____
_____
_____
_____

Take a moment to write down a few times in your life when you did not extend grace to a friend, a family member, or yourself. What will you do differently now that you know to extend grace?

Reflection:_____

_____
_____
_____
_____
_____
_____
_____
_____

PLANTING NEW GOALS IN THE SOIL OF YOUR PURPOSE, WATERED WITH DETERMINATION, BLOOMS GREATNESS.

DR. ALBERTA BROWN GREEN

Chapter Three

Creating New Goals

"Goals are put in place to lead you to your future self, who wants to meet you! Will you answer the call?"
– Dr. ABG

In chapter two, we discussed that achieving success in one's career and life depends on consistent creation and execution of goals. As you learned in chapter two, goals provide direction, clarity, and a clear path to navigate your life and the world around you.

Goals provide us with motivation, drive, and strategy to accomplish what we set out to do. Goals enhance the overall efficiency we contribute to our work, home, and lives.

True focus, drive, and meaning in our lives take place when we align ourselves with goals and resolutions that speak to who we are and what we hope to be and have in the future. Goals provide a road map of how you will get to your destination of success.

Now that you've covered, reviewed, and analyzed your previous goals, let's dig into a few reasons why they're important and what happens when you set them for your career, family, and life.

Purpose of goal creation

Goals are important because they create focus and provide direction. Typically, when someone lacks focus, they may experience a sense of uncontrollability or a sudden halt in their life. These feelings arise due to the lack of clarity and direction. A lack of clarity and direction equals a lack of focus. That's where finding focus to create goals comes into play. The significance of having well-defined goals and objectives is critical in today's world, where change is the ultimate constant.

Goals provide continuous growth

Goals motivate you to surpass your limits. Unconsciously, your life unfolds through a series of goals that you become aware of only after they have occurred. For example, once upon a time, you lived with your parents. After graduating from high school, you likely went off to college and moved into a dorm room until your junior year. Senior year, you decided it was time to live in your very first apartment in order to live as a certified adult. After graduating from college, you landed a fantastic job with excellent pay and decent benefits. There is a lovely little subdivision ten minutes away from your new job, with a two-bedroom house you toured while you were applying for jobs. You find yourself in a pivotal moment, necessitating the deliberate planning of change. Should you stay where you are, in your one-bedroom apartment that is 45 minutes away from your new job?

Your apartment is cozy and cheap, but every time friends and family stay over, it's pretty crowded, and the only places available for sleep are the recliner (your apartment doesn't have room for a couch) or the bathtub—yes, the bathtub. However, are you ready to embrace the increased financial responsibility of moving into a house? Would additional space be beneficial for you? Is it time to make the transition from apartment to house?

If you were in this situation and mostly answered yes to the questions, it would be time to stretch beyond your comfort zone and begin setting goals that will help you move into a subdivision with charming houses featuring two bedrooms and a living area spacious enough for both your recliner and couch. And the best part is that the subdivision is located just 10 minutes away from your worksite, instead of 45 minutes.

Goals keep you anchored during tough times

Life doesn't always go as planned. Loss of a job, illness of a loved one, or a cancer diagnosis always seems to come at the worst possible time. For instance, after finally being promoted to the position you've always known you've deserved, you are so excited and feel as if you are floating on cloud nine! The first thing you do is purchase the house of your dreams. Six months later, your boss calls you into his office and tells you that the company's CEO has decided to enter into an acquisition, and your position has been eliminated.

What would be your plan to stay anchored, build resilience, and move forward during this tough time?

Reflections:

_____

_____

_____

_____

After twenty-five years of teaching, you've turned in your very last piece of paperwork, and you are officially retired! Now it is time to live out the bucket list you and your husband created 15 years ago. He is so excited that you are finally free to live a retirement life with him. After three weeks of retirement, you are seated on the back porch, reading and awaiting the cup of coffee he typically brings you each morning at 6:30 a.m. It is now 7:45 am, so you get up to go and check on him and find him unresponsive. The love of your life has just had a massive stroke, and just like that, you become a full-time caregiver.

What would be your plan to stay anchored, build resilience, and move forward during this tough time?

Reflections:

_____

_____

_____

Lastly, you finally met the love of your life, who happens to check all of the boxes on a list that you wrote over ten years ago that has been tucked away in a memory box stored at the top of your closet. After your wedding day, you both instantly decide to try for children because both of you have always dreamed of having a large family. You had your annual check-up last week, which included bloodwork, a breast exam, and a Pap smear. The nurse called and left a message that the doctor wanted to review your results in person. You thought to yourself, "This is strange." While in the doctor's office, waiting for him to deliver whatever news he has, you are trying your best to stay positive. The door opens, and the doctor greets you with, "I regret to inform you, but your test results are showing that you have cervical cancer."

What would be your plan to stay anchored, build resilience, and move forward during this tough time?

Reflections:

_____

_____

_____

_____

_____

_____

Challenging issues when goals are not present

The scenarios mentioned previously would be challenging and nearly impossible to navigate without a plan and a goal. Challenging issues can drain a person's motivation and cause them to feel overwhelmed, unmotivated, and exhausted. When my clients share that their motivation levels are at an all-time low, I always ask them, "What do you think caused your motivation to tank?" Their responses range from feeling stuck, being stressed, burned out, having trouble on their job, being fearful of making big moves because they don't want to fail, and being worried about their children's challenges or their own marital issues.

One client told me their life seems to be spiraling out of control, like a merry-go-round without brakes. And another client shared that they feel as if procrastination owns them, and their life is a cycle of last-minute attempts to keep their head above water.

When life gets tough, your goals and a solid plan can serve as a lifeline through life's chaotic ups and downs. Your lifeline will be a needed compass to keep you motivated, even when setbacks threaten to knock you off the course of life. Goals define direction, and a solid plan lays the foundational steps to follow. When trouble comes knocking at your door, the goals you set and the plan you developed will keep you motivated to stay the course.

Different types of goals

Just as we have different types of shoes for various occasions—such as flip-flops for the beach, tennis shoes for walking or running, and dress shoes for special outings—we also need different types of goals to navigate life's transitions. Not all goals are created equal. To navigate grit, resilience, and accomplishment, it helps to understand the strengths of different types of goals. Three common goals are SMART goals, zone goals, and outcome goals. Each serves a distinct purpose—whether you're desiring structure, seeking focus, or chasing big dreams.

By applying the right type of goal at the right moment, you can align your desire with focus and improve both your performance and satisfaction. Let's explore what makes each of these goals important and how they can work together to move you forward with purpose!

SMART goals

SMART goals are exactly what they are called—smart. There is no mystery, secrets, or confusion. SMART goals have been around since the early 1980s. SMART goals were introduced as a practical method for setting clear and effective objectives. Over time, it became a widely adopted framework in business, education, and personal development. SMART goals help maintain focus while completing achievable goals.

If you are the type of person who thinks in black and white, likes to get straight to the point, and enjoys step-by-step directions with no fluff, SMART goals are for you. SMART goals are clear, defined, and structured. They lead you straight to the endpoint—no mystery about how you will make it to the end. SMART goals will make you feel like you are a planner or project manager. SMART goals help you to move from "someday I will go back to school" to "I will go back to school on August 17, 2025, and graduate in May of 2029."

Take a moment to write out your thoughts about how you could utilize SMART goals for your future goal planning.
*Reflections:*_____

_____
_____
_____
_____
_____
_____
_____
_____
_____
_____
_____
_____

Outcome goals

Outcome goals are called end-game goals. They are high-profile, loud, and flashy. Outcome goals are powerful and inspirational, and they help set your vision for competitive situations. Outcome goals can be bold but tricky because they depend on outside factors you can't control, like surprise illness, a sudden unwanted change to your career, or other people's decisions.

Examples of outcome goals are losing twenty pounds in twenty days, getting promoted by January (you were just hired in November), finding a spouse in the next four months, and running a marathon in under four hours." Outcome goals can be thought of as the title of your book, and the chapters can be considered your daily actions to complete the goals.

Outcome goals are good to set when you need to pull a rabbit out of the hat—meaning you want to accomplish something that is inspirational and amazing! You seek a win that will change your life or take you to the next level of success. Outcome goals can be compared to vision boards. Think about it… do you ever put something simple and easy on your vision board? No, you don't. When creating a vision board, you place your BIG hopes, dreams, and desires in written and pictorial form on it. These outcome goals make your vision come to life!

However, while outcome goals are exciting, motivating, and emotionally charged, they can be extremely fragile because they are high on desire and hope and low on control of outcome.

Some people call outcome goals wishful thinking, but I beg to differ because when you pair them with proper planning and focus, there is a high probability of crossing the finish line with success of reaching your goal.

Take a moment to write out your thoughts about how you could utilize outcome goals for your future goal planning.
*Reflections:*_____

_____
_____
_____
_____
_____
_____
_____
_____
_____
_____
_____

Zone Goals

Zone goals keep you grounded in the moment and teach you to focus on your behavior and the effort you put forth to complete the goal rather than its outcome. For example, instead of saying "make an A on the test," a zone goal would be "show up for class, ask the professor for help if needed, and study until it's time for the test." Zone goals are wonderful for perfectionists and overachievers because zone goals keep them from connecting their self-worth to whether or not they accomplish their goals. For instance, if a person is constantly winning at everything they do, but an outside circumstance or unrealistic expectation causes them to not win or complete the goal, they may be overly disappointed in themselves. Zone goals keep you focused on what you have the ability to control—your thoughts, the process, and your decisions.

While outcome goals require winning and being on top, zone goals allow you to be in the moment, breathe, and enjoy the ride. They're rooted in the now, leaning on consistency rather than perfection.

Zone goals are rooted in mindfulness, patience, and mastery. They're ideal for high-pressure situations where the final outcomes can be derailed by overthinking. Zone goals are setting your sights on experiencing the process versus the end goal. Zone goals help you to relax and do your best.

Zone goals can be broken down into three categories: outrageous goals, ambitious goals, and attainable goals. Outrageous goals are the ambitious targets you set for yourself, which may lead others to believe you've lost your mind, and you might even question your own sanity. An example of an outrageous goal would be becoming a social media influencer when you have only one platform and you post once in a blue moon. However, you saw a few heartfelt clips from an influencer that you follow, so you said to yourself, "I think I can do that." Next thing you know, you wrote on your vision board that you would become a top-paid social media influencer with over 1 million followers within six months or less.

An ambitious goal can be achieved with time, effort, and a little elbow grease. Another example of an ambitious goal is saving up enough money to take your first cruise in the next six months. The cruise costs $499.99. It will be challenging, but you have committed to shaving off a few items on your budget in order to save for your cruise. So, you've decided to forego your monthly nail appointment, daily Starbucks run, and pause your Netflix subscription for the next six months.

Lastly, an attainable goal is a goal you can do with minimal effort. You complete attainable goals with little to no effort.

Examples of attainable goals are brushing your teeth, going to work on time, going to bed early, and eating breakfast in the morning.

Take a moment to write out your thoughts about how you could utilize zone goals (outrageous goals, ambitious goals, and attainable goals) for your future goal planning.

*Reflections:*_____
_____
_____
_____
_____
_____
_____
_____
_____
_____
_____
_____
_____
_____
_____
_____

Let's create new goals

Now that we've vetted through SMART, OUTCOME, and ZONE GOALS, it's time for you to create new goals. If you are having trouble creating your new goals, you may utilize some of the goals covered in Chapter Two, which are goals most people strive for every year.

I've listed the categories below to choose from:
1. health and fitness
2. personal development
3. professional development/career/education
4. financial
5. relationship and social
6. mental and emotional well-being

Health and fitness goals may include weight loss, regular exercise, eating a balanced and nutritious diet, getting more sleep, or reducing stress. They can also include building consistent routines, improving mobility and strength, or committing to regular checkups and preventive care.

Personal development goals may consist of reading more, learning new skills or hobbies, managing your time more effectively, setting aside time for self-care, or taking online courses and attending professional development workshops.

Professional development and career goals help people aspire to advance in their current job or seek a new career opportunity. Starting a business, improving work-life balance, and expanding professional networks are other aspirations.

People seeking to enhance their educational goals seek to further their education, build marketable skills, gain new certifications, and find mentors in their field of study who can open doors and offer guidance.

Financial goals give your money purpose and direction. Common examples include saving money, building an emergency fund, paying off debt, and creating and sticking to a budget; longer-term goals often include investing for retirement, funding education, or establishing multiple income streams to increase long-term security.

Relationship and social goals focus on strengthening connections, creating meaningful experiences, and contributing to the lives of others. Examples include scheduling regular quality time with family, hosting monthly friend gatherings, calling or messaging loved ones more consistently, and planning purposeful dates that deepen partnerships. These goals also cover community engagement, such as volunteering with a local nonprofit, mentoring someone, joining a club or faith group, and organizing or participating in service projects.

Lastly, mental and emotional well-being goals are essential for maintaining balance, clarity, and inner peace as you pursue your larger life objectives. These goals may include reducing screen time, practicing a digital detox, seeking therapy or counseling, and cultivating gratitude and positive thinking.

Now that you have a few examples of new goals and their descriptions, take a moment to write down your new goals. List your goals with space between each one so you can write how you'll achieve them. Writing out your thoughts regarding how you will complete the goal provides stability to your process.

*Reflections:*_____

_____
_____
_____
_____
_____
_____
_____
_____
_____
_____
_____
_____
_____

STRATEGY IS THE BRIDGE THAT MOVES YOUR GOAL FROM THE STARTING LINE TO FINISHING STRONG.

DR. ALBERTA BROWN GREEN

Chapter Four

Add Strategy to Your Goals

"A goal is a wonderful thing to create. However, a goal is merely a thought if you don't create a plan to achieve it."
– Dr. ABG

Now that you have your goals, let's wrap a strategy around them. "A goal without a plan is just a wishful thought." People who write down goals are 42% more likely to complete them. However, if you don't have a strategy behind your goals, it will be tough to make it to the finish line.

Goals coupled with strategy are easier to achieve within a strategic time frame and with available resources. Strategy supplies the sequence of steps, timelines, and resources needed to make that wish real. In other words, strategy gives you the ability to do what you said you would do!

Defining a strategy for your goals

A strategy is a specific plan you'll use to meet objectives to accomplish your goals. Strategy helps to set specific objectives and break down goals into more explicit directions by providing quantitative measurements. Because goals are broad, you need certain strategies to define, accomplish, and reach the goal (final outcome). For instance, we talked about outcome goals that are centered around the desired result or achievement. There are three types of outcome goals: short-term, mid-term, and long-term. Short-term goals are goals you can complete daily or within a few weeks or months. Mid-term goals can last between twelve months to two years. And long-term goals take several years or even decades. These three types of outcome goals can help you set the tone for your strategy.

Defining a strategy for your goals helps to keep you motivated and sane. Without a strategy for your goals, dreams can float around like leaves falling from a tree during a windy fall day – beautiful to watch but hard to catch in your hands.

A good strategy allows you to break down your goals into palatable, bite-sized to-do lists and assign realistic deadlines that won't send you into a paralyzed state of languishing (stuck) – not able to move forward due to the magnitude of the goal. Instead, strategy helps you to move forward, track progress, and actually be able to say, I DID IT!!! I accomplished my amazing, big, hairy, audacious goal!

Furthermore, a good strategy is like adding ranch dressing to your salad – it enhances the flavor and taste of the cucumbers, lettuce, tomatoes, and cheese, bringing it all together. Basically, strategy is the secret sauce you sprinkle on your amazing, big, hairy, audacious dreams to turn them into real-life achievements.

Lastly, think of strategy as the GPS guiding you from "I'd like to get over my fear of flying" to "Wow, I've just landed in Vegas and I've conquered my fear of flying." It maps out the route, sets pit stops for breaks, and warns you when you're about to take a wrong exit into a black hole of social media binge land. Or, strategy politely stops you from thinking that you can write an entire twelve-chapter book in a weekend, after watching an info-commercial or a YouTube video that said this could with their help, for a small fee of $49.99.

What are your thoughts about strategy?
*Reflections:*_____

_____
_____
_____
_____
_____
_____
_____
_____
_____
_____
_____
_____
_____

Strategy in practice

When you wrap strategy around your goals, it makes completing long-term goals bearable and challenging goals fun. Let's practice adding strategy to your goals.

Have you heard the old saying of "How do you eat an elephant? You eat it one bite at a time."

Today, let's put a strategy around eating an elephant. Before we get started, this is just an example.

Putting strategy around the "eat an elephant one bite at a time" quote means transforming a big, intimidating goal into an understandable, step-by-step strategy or plan. Instead of facing an enormous goal or challenge that paralyzes you, you define your goal with a defined process that breaks it into digestible bites. Next, you will assign each bite a purpose and a timeline. This approach turns anxiety into action, feeling overwhelmed into order, and turns every mini win into proof that you're constantly making progress toward the finish line.

Adding strategy to your goals isn't just about breaking them into bite-sized portions; it also means tracking your progress, resetting your plan when you need to, and celebrating not only reaching the finish line of your goal, but throughout the process. For example, if you want to eat an elephant, create small checkpoints to see how much you've eaten, think about how you can eat more smoothly next time, and give yourself a little reward after each bite to stay motivated.

Keep doing what helps you and stop what doesn't. That way, you make steady progress and build the confidence to tackle even the biggest goals.

Below are steps to help you build a strategy around your plan to eat an elephant (reach our goals).

Define the Elephant (Goal) – Decide exactly what your big goal is. What is the goal? Why do you want to accomplish this goal? What does it look like to successfully complete this goal? And pin down what "finished" looks like, so each bite has a clear target.

Break it into bites – Break down the big goal into smaller, standalone tasks. Shoot for portions that can be completed within a few days or weeks, so the momentum to complete the goal remains high.

Organize your bites – Place your bites (tasks) in order of most important to least important. Next, create a timeline or roadmap that takes you from the first most important bite to the last. Throughout your important bites, sprinkle in the least important, easy bites, to aid in your small wins.

Check, pivot, and adapt – Establish checkpoints to track your bite-sized progress. This will help you to see how you are doing. After each checkpoint, review what went well, adjust your plan if needed, and refine your next steps.

Celebrate each bite (Goal) – Create mini-rewards to acknowledge each stand-alone task. In other words, give yourself a treat or a pat on the back when you finish a task. Recognizing progress not only reinforces positive habits to keep you going but also sustains the energy needed to eat the whole elephant (finish the goal).

Take a moment and choose a goal that has been challenging to complete. Now write it down below and walk through the process we just reviewed.

*Reflections:*_____
_____
_____
_____
_____
_____
_____
_____
_____
_____
_____
_____
_____
_____

When you're staring down at a big dream or a huge goal, it can feel overwhelming at first, like you're not even sure where to start. But when you slow down and define what success looks like for you, not what somebody else thinks it should be, you give yourself a clear picture of the finish line. Then, instead of trying to swallow the whole elephant at once, you break it down into small, manageable bites. Those little steps build momentum, and before you know it, the thing that once felt impossible is already in motion.

The key is layering in strategy—being intentional about what you tackle first and not just throwing effort in every direction. When you prioritize your tasks on a timeline and sprinkle in some quick, easy wins, you give yourself the fuel to keep going when the bigger pieces take longer. It's like giving yourself little checkpoints that remind you, *"Hey, I'm making progress."* And that progress builds confidence. Whether it takes days, weeks, or years, staying steady with those steps guarantees success. It's not about speed, it's about direction, persistence, and remembering that every bite you take moves you closer to the goal you set out to crush.

In summary, with a strategy, it is possible to eat an elephant, one bite at a time. By defining exactly what success looks like, followed by breaking it into bite-sized tasks, you can accomplish your goals, depending on the magnitude of the goal, in a few days, weeks, months, or years.

Adding strategy, by prioritizing tasks on a timeline, weaving in quick, easy wins to keep you moving toward the finish line, will lead you to guaranteed success. Let's pretend you would like to write a book. Use the ***strategy below to keep your goals consistent.***

Tip 1: **Clearly define the goal** – Instead of "I want to write a book", say "I will create a writing timeline with milestones to finish my book in October of next year".

Tip 2: **Divide goals into milestone steps** – Your steps to write a book could include creating chapter titles, outlining the chapter titles, writing 400 words a day, and completing a draft of the book by a set date.

Tip 3: **Assign time** – Schedule time on your calendar for each milestone. Commit to the time, and don't cancel your appointment.

Tip 4: **Track progress and pivot** – Monitor your progress, make necessary changes, and celebrate your small wins. Be willing to adjust your strategy if needed.

Tip 5: **Hold yourself accountable** – Share your goal with a family member or trusted friend. Check in with this person and share your progress. Regular check-ins will help you stay motivated and encourage you to keep going.

MOTIVATION IS THE SPARK THAT LIGHTS THE PATH TO ACHIEVING YOUR GREATEST DREAMS.

DR. ALBERTA BROWN GREEN

Chapter Five

Motivate Yourself

"Your motivation is your responsibility, and you get to set the tone for your mindset and message to yourself."
- Dr. ABG

The art of self-motivation

Self-motivation comes from within and pushes you to take action and pursue goals without being pressured or needing external rewards. When you're stuck—waking up feeling hopeless, watching opportunities slip by, or repeating the same old routines—it's easy to look for someone or something else to motivate you.

Tapping into self-motivation helps you reclaim ownership of your day-to-day choices and your life. Even small commitments—like setting a 15-minute "start" timer or celebrating the completion of a single task—become powerful tools to remind you that you can move forward on your own schedule. Creating your own motivation doesn't just help you break free from inactivity; it helps you choose how you will command your morning, manage your day, and how you will treat and talk to yourself. Basically, self-motivation rewires how you operate in life and how you see challenges.

For instance, rather than viewing obstacles and challenges as being stuck, each hurdle becomes an opportunity to be positive, prove your adaptability to pivot, and encourage yourself to push through.

As you learn to motivate yourself by building momentum with tiny successes such as completing that book, joining a dating app, or taking a short walk, you begin to see yourself as someone who overcomes, not someone who allows life to pass them by. Over time, these daily acts of moving forward stack up, transforming "I can't" into "I did," and shine a light on the darkness of procrastination and propel you into new possibilities.

On a scale of 1-10, where is your motivation, and why did you choose that number?

*Reflections:*_____

_____

_____

_____

_____

_____

_____

_____

_____

When self-motivation is nonexistent

For some, self-motivation is difficult to conjure up out of thin air, let alone manage. I've even heard people say you either have it or you don't, as if it were a fixed trait handed out at birth. When people lack motivation, they often procrastinate, miss planned engagements, feel overwhelmed, and struggle to make consistent progress toward their goals or certain activities that deal with life in general. When motivation is missing, days may feel heavy and tasks seem to pile up. Even small, easy choices cause unneeded stress and become difficult to complete. Your interests disappear, and responsibility goes out the window.

The lack of motivation may stem from unclear goals, exhaustion, the fear of starting, perfectionism, or the feeling of a heavy burden of unfinished tasks or amounts of work. Without motivation, a person is slow to make decisions, daily necessary routines suffer, and isolation creeps in and opens the door for self-criticism.

Signs of nonexistent motivation

When motivation is nonexistent, there are usually signs of persistent avoidance, low energy, and shrinking enjoyment. When you were asked earlier, 'Where is your motivation on a scale of 1-10, and why did you choose that number?' the intention was to set the tone to help you describe your experience with your level of motivation.

Naming your experience makes it easier to talk about. Putting words to what you feel and why it matters turns a vague problem into a concrete one you can address. Once you can describe the barrier, you can choose a small, specific action to begin reversing it.

    Let's meet Maranda, who has nonexistent motivation. Maranda is 32 years old and hasn't had a weekend to herself in over five years. Her hair seems unkept, as if she styled it in less than one minute. She appears tired, overwhelmed, and spaced out. I observed Maranda and her children in Walmart – I don't know her personally, but overheard her name during a conversation with her friend. I guess you can say that I was being nosy. While standing in line, I watched all three of Maranda's kids run around touching everything, while screaming and laughing at the top of their lungs. They were terrorizing the person in front of them by pushing the buggy into the back of their heels. Her friend said, "Maranda, are you going to do something with your kids?" Maranda looked at her friend, shook her head side to side, and responded, "I have no motivation. I'm just here going through the motions".

    Maranda is a recently divorced, now single mother of three active kiddos. She is currently working two jobs and is battling acute depression and anxiety. She wants to stop her children from terrorizing the lady in front of them, but she can't due to her lack of motivation and stress. She barely mustered up the energy to drive to the grocery store.

What are the signs of Maranda's nonexistent motivation?
Reflections:_____

_____

_____

Motivation keeps you moving forward in life

Remember when you were younger? Motivation is your mom opening your bedroom door and saying, "Why haven't you cleaned this dirty room? Once you finish cleaning it, then you can go out with your friends tonight, and if you don't, you and I will watch Netflix." To avoid three sappy Netflix movies in a row and miss out on hanging out with your friends, you are now motivated to complete the goal of cleaning your room.

As a grown-up, motivation is like getting a call at 8 am on Saturday that your friend is coming to town, and you haven't seen her in over five years! There is no way you can cancel or make up an excuse, right? So, your friend and her family will be arriving at your home around 1:00 pm-ish. However, it looks as if a bomb exploded in the living room. Let's not discuss the fact that you have enough dog hair on the floor to knit three small toddler sweaters with matching hats, the kitchen is a hot dirty mess, and the sink has dishes in it that haven't been washed in almost a week.

You have no clean towels, the kids' rooms... let's not even talk about it, and worst of all, you are out of paper towels, toilet paper, and your secret chocolate stash (don't judge), because you haven't been able to visit Sam's Club in a few weeks. However, you refuse to allow your friend, the person who comments on people's baseboards, to see you living like a filthy bum, so you wake everyone up and torture (motivate) them to help you clean until the house looks like an Airbnb.

Different types of motivation

Motivation is when a person has a general desire and willingness to initiate change and maintain goal-oriented behaviors. Sometimes the change can be quick, like having to clean up in a few hours before company arrives, or long-term, like having to stay on course with healthy eating and exercise habits to lower your risk of diabetes, which may run in your family. Let's talk about three types of motivation—intrinsic, extrinsic, and integrated motivation.

Intrinsic motivation comes from within oneself. There is a deep internal desire to accomplish a great task that fills you with purpose – you were born to complete this mission. When people are driven by internal rewards—such as curiosity, mastery, or meaning—they're not just checking boxes; they're fully immersed in the process and allow all their creativity to flow, rarely having a backup plan.

On the other hand, ***extrinsic motivation*** deals with receiving external rewards. This desire arises outside of oneself. There is an external situation that causes the motivation—money, prestige, fame, and accomplishment in the eyes of others. Some individuals seek external motivation to avoid various forms of punishment. For instance, you arrive at work on time to avoid being fired, or you feel compelled to keep a job that you dislike because your wife and kids depend on you for food, insurance, and shelter. Relying solely on external motivation is like pedaling with training wheels—it gets you moving but never teaches you to ride solo.

Integrated regulation motivation sits comfortably between internal and external motivation. It's like being invited to exercise with a friend as their plus one, but over time, you come to enjoy it and purchase your own membership because you now enjoy working out. Integrated regulation motivation lives in the middle of "I have to do this" and "I desire to do this," where external incentives slowly transition to your personal values until the activity feels—as if by fate—entirely your own. Think of it as motivation dipping its toe in the water, only to eventually dive full into the water!

Using all three types of motivation to move forward

Now that you have a good understanding of extrinsic motivation, intrinsic motivation, and integrated regulation motivation, begin with extrinsic motivation to create certain awards, set deadlines, and use accountability to get yourself moving. Then build integrated regulation by connecting the task to your values and identity so it feels more personal and important. Finally, increase your intrinsic motivation by scheduling regular time for learning, exploring your interests, and doing the tasks in ways that feel meaningful, which makes your progress enjoyable and long-lasting.

Self-Motivation Tips

To jumpstart your motivation meter, below are three tips to get you started.

1. Create a "why" that's bigger than the work.

When your reason is personal and powerful—something that connects to your values or the future you want—it'll pull you forward even on the hard days. Write down your "why" and keep it where you can see it daily.

2. Celebrate progress, not just outcomes.

Don't wait until you hit the big goal to feel proud. Notice and reward yourself for the small steps: finishing a task, keeping a promise to yourself, or choosing discipline over comfort. Each win proves you're moving in the right direction.

3. Speak to yourself like you would a friend.

Self-talk can either drain you or drive you. Instead of saying "I can't do this," flip it to "I'm learning how to do this." Encourage yourself with the same kindness and belief you'd give someone you love—because your own words are fuel.

Now that you understand the art of self-motivation—when it falters, how to reignite it, the three types of motivation, and practical tips to keep your motivation meter moving—I'll guide you through my favorite motivation techniques and concrete suggestions to elevate your drive to the next level.

Morning Mindshift

If you want to jumpstart your motivation, try a morning mindshift. Did you know you were created to rise with the sun? Our bodies reflect this order through circadian rhythms, which naturally align with sunrise and sunset. Rising with the sun not only honors this built-in design for our body but also fuels productivity and focus, setting a confident tone for the day.

Personally, I rise every morning at 4:30 a.m. Aligning my energy with sunlight grounds me before my work begins. Also, rising early provides a sense of freedom to gently ease into my day. No one is asking me questions; there is a quiet energy in my surroundings, and my thoughts are so clear. My mornings consist of prayer and meditation, a hot shower, a hot cup of coffee or tea poured into my favorite mug, listening to worship music, and enjoying the stillness of morning. After prayer and meditation, I exercise, and lastly, I create a five-item task list, personal and work-related, and challenge myself to complete at least one task from each list before I walk out the door. Just think, I've already accomplished two small victories before arriving to work at 8:00 am.

Morning Mindshift Suggestion: The moment you get up, do not reach for your phone—instead, head straight to the bathroom to release yesterday's waste. Yes, really—pee and do number two. Bathe, wash your face and all body parts—even feet—and brush and floss your teeth. While doing this, literally and metaphorically, feel the waste, clutter, and dirt leave your body. Allow the water to cleanse you. Next, spend five to ten minutes stretching or practicing gentle yoga. Feel your muscles awaken as blood flows through tired, tight, or worn joints. This simple movement jumpstarts your circulation, sharpens your mind, and signals to your body that today is an opportunity, not an obligation.

Lastly, carve out a brief gratitude ritual. Grab a journal and list three things you appreciate in this very moment. Writing down small wins—a warm bed, a friend's text, a roof over your head—anchors your mindset in abundance rather than lack, creating momentum to achieve bigger goals.

What are a few additional activities you could add to your morning Mindshift activities?
*Reflections:*_____

_____
_____
_____
_____

Intentional Movement

Your body requires intentional movement to function and stay alive. Your organs, blood flow, muscles, and even a bowel movement will operate and function with intentional movement. Body movement can consist of stretching your muscles, walking, cleaning up your house, and even breathing. If you have a desk job or a sedentary lifestyle, you must be intentional with moving your body.

Intentional Movement Suggestions: Incorporate brief movement breaks throughout your day. Research shows even five minutes of light exercise—stretching, a short walk, or desk yoga—boosts blood flow, sharpens focus, and uplifts mood. Treat each break as a mini reset button for both body and mind. Schedule these bursts of activity before or after tasks you find draining. For example, stand up, stretch, and perform calf raises every 30 minutes of work. Over time, these small pauses transform into energy anchors that carry you through long days with greater resilience. Use music to power your movement rituals. Create a "move" playlist of two- to three-minute tracks that signal it's time to get up. As soon as the beat drops, drop whatever you're doing and let your body respond—this auditory cue cements the habit. Consider bringing a pair of comfortable tennis shoes to work and keeping them at your desk. By doing this, you make it easy to take short walks and stretch breaks without disrupting your day or feet!

Lastly, reflect on how you feel after the movement. Keep a quick log of your energy levels before and after each break. Noticing the consistency of these boosts will motivate you to maintain and even expand your movement practice.

What are your thoughts on Morning Mindshift and Intentional Movement?

*Reflections:*_____
_____
_____
_____
_____
_____
_____
_____

Water Consumption and Usage

Water is heaven's touch and blessing to the body. We lived our first nine months in a fluid state, and our bodies are about eighty percent water. Drinking water cleanses us from the inside and out, supporting cell nutrition, waste removal, joint protection, and temperature regulation. With most bodily processes relying on it, water truly is the ultimate elixir. Without water, we could not survive more than three days.

Water Consumption and Usage Suggestions: Start your day with a tall glass of water. If you have trouble drinking water, place two bottles of water on your nightstand and two bottles of water at your work desk. When you rise, drink a full bottle of water from your nightstand, and drink the other bottle before you go to sleep. As for the two bottles that you will take to work, drink one bottle once you arrive at work, and drink the other bottle before you leave work. In addition to placing the bottles of water on your nightstand and at your work desk, consider carrying a reusable water bottle as your constant companion. Aim for eight glasses of water a day, but listen to your body—if you feel sluggish or notice dark urine, drink more water. Staying hydrated not only elevates energy but also enhances concentration and mood.

    As for the outside of your body, in the mornings, take a refreshing shower to wash away yesterday. In the evening, soak in a warm bath with Epsom salts to relax muscles and soothe the mind.

    Transform drinking water into a mindful practice. Infuse your water with slices of lemon, cucumber, or mint. Sip slowly, noticing each sensation. This intentional pause brings calm to your morning and reminds you that self-care can be as simple as a glass of water. Lastly, always drink a full bottle of water before your coffee consumption. Coffee is a diuretic, and if you only drink coffee all day, you can become dehydrated.

What are other ways to increase your water consumption and usage?

Reflections:_____

_____

_____

_____

_____

Journal Reflection

Journaling your thoughts is deeply therapeutic. Writing freely, without judgment or editing, allows raw ideas to flow. Allowing raw ideas to flow surfaces hidden beliefs and emotional patterns that influence motivation. Over time, you'll spot recurring themes—strengths to build on and obstacles to address. Ask yourself questions at the end of each reflection to clarify what you learned.

Journaling Suggestions: Dedicate time each morning or evening to your thoughts. Date each journal entry. Start with three prompts: What went well today? What challenged me? What's one thing I'll improve tomorrow? This practice transforms adding dates to your experiences into purposeful insights. Once a week, review your entries for patterns. Highlight phrases that repeatedly appear, whether positive ("I felt energized") or negative ("I kept procrastinating"). Use these cues to adjust strategies—double down on what works and retool what doesn't.

Lastly, end your reflection with a short, forward-looking statement by writing, "Tomorrow, I choose to…" This final line shifts focus from past to future, prepping your mind for proactive, motivated action.

What are your thoughts about journal reflection? Are there other actions you can do to enhance your journaling time?
*Reflections:*_____

_____

_____

_____

_____

Affirmations

Affirmations are powerful statements that motivate you to stay in a positive headspace. What positive message will you tell yourself today? Stand in front of the mirror and declare, "I am capable, I am resilient, and today will be a great day." Let gratitude flow by naming three blessings—big or small—that fuel your spirit right now. Next, ask: whose day can I brighten? Send a quick text of encouragement or offer a genuine compliment to the person who comes to mind. These two simple acts—affirming yourself and uplifting another—create a ripple of motivation that carries you both forward.

Affirmation Suggestions: Craft your affirmations in the present tense and avoid negatives. Instead of saying, "I am not afraid," choose "I face challenges with courage." Infuse each statement with feeling—let your voice rise with conviction to rewire deep-seated beliefs. Combine affirmations with journaling. Write each line slowly, noticing how it lands in your heart and mind. Revisit these notes at night to track your evolving self-talk and celebrate the small shifts in confidence you've gained while speaking encouragement, positivity, and life over yourself.

What are three additional affirmations you can tell yourself?
Reflections: _____

_____

_____

_____

_____

Visualization

Visualization means vividly imagining yourself as the person you want to become, a clearer, stronger version of who you are. Did you know your brain can't tell the difference between a real achievement and a highly detailed mental rehearsal?

Visualization Suggestions: To practice visualization, close your eyes each morning and picture your goals in vivid detail. Feel the thankfulness and joy of achieving them—the smells, the sounds, the applause. After you envision reaching the goal, anchor that vision with action. Write down one step you can take today toward your goal. Keep that note somewhere visible—on your bathroom mirror, at your office desk, or next to your nightstand where you keep your water bottle—to remind yourself that visualization demands follow-through! Another suggestion is to experiment with guided visualization audio. There are short tracks that walk you through success scenarios, from delivering a presentation to crossing a marathon finish line. Listening while relaxed deepens the mental imprint and fuels your belief in possibility.

Lastly, create a vision board or a simple collage of images that represent your objectives. Place it where you'll see it often—on your desk or phone wallpaper. Each glance reignites your focus, turning abstract wishes into concrete reminders of what you're striving for.

What is a hope or dream you will envision yourself reaching and accomplishing?
*Reflections:*_____

_____
_____
_____
_____

Advice for self-motivation

A piece of advice that has followed me throughout life is "Don't waste a single moment worrying about what hasn't been done – start where you are". Your motivation is your responsibility, and you get to set the tone for your mindset and message to yourself. You have the power to decide when to move forward. Remember the tools you've learned in this chapter, whether it's intentional movement, morning mind shift, affirmations, or visualization, were shared to enhance your motivation. Use these tips not just as last-minute tricks, but as daily motivation to speak kindly and confidently to yourself, as well as encouragement to move forward. Every morning, choose a positive message—"I can," "I will," "Let's go"—and watch how your tone shapes your actions.

Crushing your goals and increasing your motivation doesn't demand perfection; it demands presence. Instead of fixating on the mountain of what you haven't accomplished, motivate yourself to plant your feet firmly where you stand right now and take a single, deliberate step forward. Lean on the tips we covered—maybe that's diving headfirst into creating your morning mind shift, positive self-talk, and visualizing yourself being motivated to do what you said you would do. Each small action builds motivation, and motivation is the secret ingredient that turns your "one day" into "day one," and your "someday" into "today."

Finally, surround yourself with people who match your desired motivation and energy. Trust me....being around motivated and positive people changes your outlook for the better. Your circle should include those who celebrate progress, share honest feedback, and keep you moving forward even on tough days. Surround yourself with friends who remind you of your "why" when you feel unmotivated, and mentors who push you to go beyond your comfort zone. Motivation isn't a solo sport — it's a shared rhythm. When you choose companions with can-do attitudes, you amplify your own drive and finish strong together.

Who are a few people whom you admire, regarding their motivational drive? What additional actions will you take to motivate yourself to keep going and striving?

*Reflections:*_____

_____

_____

_____

_____

_____

_____

_____

CONSISTENCY IS HAVING A STEADY FLOW OF PROGRESS, NO MATTER HOW BIG OR SMALL, TAKING YOU FROM NOW TO YOUR FUTURE SUCCESS.

DR. ALBERTA BROWN GREEN

Chapter Six

Commit to Consistency

"When and how you show up in life and work depends on Consistency".

- Dr. ABG

You were created to be consistent. From the rhythm of your heartbeat to the cycles of nature, your design is rooted in reliability. Your potential thrives in structure, and your spirit finds peace in alignment. When you operate in consistency, you're not forcing something unnatural—you're returning to your original blueprint. You were made to be dependable, resilient, and intentional. It's not just what you do—it's who you are. The more you honor that truth, the more empowered you become to live it out.

Consistency is not a personality trait—it's a decision. A discipline. A declaration of intent. Consistency is being committed to choosing alignment over impulse and purpose over procrastination. It's the quiet power behind every breakthrough, the steady rhythm that transforms goals into realities. When we commit to showing up—especially when it's inconvenient—we begin to build a life that reflects our values, not just our moods.

Consistency in Action

Consistency is the bridge between who we are and who we're becoming. It's not glamorous, but it's transformational. And it's available to anyone willing to choose it daily.

Many people know what to do. They've read the books, attended the workshops, listened to the podcasts. But knowing is not the same as doing. The gap between knowledge and action is where most dreams don't come to fruition. Bridging that gap requires activating the full self—mind, body, and spirit. The mind must be focused, the body disciplined, and the spirit anchored in belief. When these three work in harmony, action becomes expected. It's not just about having the right information—it's about embodying it, living it, and letting it shape your daily decisions. Consistency is the vehicle that carries knowledge into motion.

Now that we have a good understanding of consistency, let's get to work! In order to follow through with consistency, you must anchor your actions to purpose, create systems for your goals, celebrate your wins, protect your environment, and embrace progress over perfection.

Anchor your actions to purpose

Consistency becomes sustainable when it's rooted in something deeper than obligation. When your daily actions are connected to a clear purpose—whether it's personal growth, community impact, or spiritual alignment, they gain meaning.

Purpose fuels perseverance. Instead of asking "What do I have to do today?" ask "What am I building toward?" This shift transforms routine into ritual and discipline into devotion. When your "why" is strong, your "how" becomes non-negotiable.

Create systems, not just goals

Goals give direction, but systems create momentum and consistency. A system is a repeatable structure that supports your desired outcome—like a morning routine, a weekly planning session, or a habit tracker. Systems reduce decision fatigue and make consistency automatic. Instead of relying on motivation, you rely on rhythm. The more you build systems around your values, the less you'll need to force consistency—it will begin to flow naturally.

Below are a few suggestions to help you create systems for consistency.

Design a Daily Anchor Routine

Start your day with a consistent set of actions that ground you—whether it's journaling, stretching, prayer, or reviewing your goals. This anchor routine doesn't need to be long; it just needs to be intentional. It sets the tone for your day and reinforces your commitment to showing up. When your mornings begin with clarity and purpose, your decisions throughout the day become more aligned and less reactive.

Schedule Weekly Reflection and Planning Time

Consistency thrives when you pause to assess and adjust. Set aside time each week to reflect on what worked, what didn't, and what needs refining. Use this space to plan your priorities, schedule your commitments, and reconnect with your goals. This system keeps your vision fresh and your actions focused. It also prevents burnout by allowing you to course-correct before anxiety or stress sets in.

How will you incorporate a daily anchor routine, and scheduled weekly reflections and planning time to help you stay consistent toward your goals?

*Reflections:*_____

_____

_____

_____

_____

Use Visual Trackers to Reinforce Progress

Whether it's a habit tracker, calendar, or checklist, visual tools help you see your consistency in action. They provide instant feedback and a sense of accomplishment. Tracking progress also builds accountability—especially when shared with a coach, peer, or group. The goal isn't perfection; it's consistency. When you see your effort, you're more likely to sustain it.

Automate What You Can, Personalize What You Must

Reduce friction by automating repetitive tasks—like meal planning, reminders, or digital workflows. This frees up mental energy for the things that require creativity and emotional investment. At the same time, personalize your systems to reflect your values and lifestyle. A system that feels rigid or irrelevant won't last. The key is to make consistency easier, not harder—by designing systems that work for you, not against you.

How will you incorporate visual trackers and automation to help you stay consistent with your goals?

*Reflections:*_____

_____

_____

Celebrate Micro-Wins

Big results are built on small victories. Recognizing and celebrating micro-wins—like completing a workout, writing a paper, or choosing a healthy meal—reinforces progress and builds confidence. These moments remind you that consistency is working, even when the finish line feels far away. Celebration isn't just about reward—it's about reflection. It helps you stay emotionally connected to your journey and fuels the desire to keep going.

How will you celebrate your Micro-wins?

Reflections: _____

_____

_____

_____

_____

<u>Task Chunking</u>

Task Chunking is great for celebrating micro-wins. Use the method of Task Chunking when goals feel overwhelming, which will stall your motivation. When Task Chunking, break each objective into micro-tasks—tiny, manageable actions you can complete in under ten minutes. Checking off these mini steps releases dopamine and propels you forward.

Start by outlining the full project, then identify logical slices: research, draft, review, and refine. Assign each slice to a specific day or time block. Watching your list shrink keeps momentum high and fear low.

Pair chunking with clear deadlines. Use a digital calendar or sticky notes to assign each micro-task a time slot. The visible schedule banishes ambiguity and primes your mind to move from intention to action. At week's end, review how many chunks you've completed. Celebrate progress regardless of pace—this weekly audit offers perspective, reminding you that small, consistent wins eclipse sporadic bursts of effort.

How will you celebrate your Micro-wins using task chunking?

*Reflections:*_____

_____

_____

_____

_____

_____

Protect Your Environment

Your surroundings profoundly affect consistency. Your surroundings either support or sabotage your consistency. That includes your physical space, digital usage, and the people you engage with. A cluttered environment breeds distraction; a toxic one breeds doubt and confusion. Create spaces that inspire focus, surround yourself with voices that uplift, and eliminate triggers that pull you off course. Consistency thrives in environments that reinforce your values and minimize resistance.

Refresh your setup regularly. At the start of each week, rearrange or clean your space for a renewed sense of ownership. This process not only preserves order but also rekindles enthusiasm as you step into a workspace that feels intentionally yours. Refresh your setup relates to your workout space, bedroom, and any location you spend a majority of your time.

Below are a few suggestions to protect your environment in order to be consistent.

- <u>Declutter your primary workspace</u>—remove items that don't serve staying committed to your current goals. A tidy desk signals a clear mind and invites focused effort.
- <u>Introduce elements that inspire you</u> – a motivational quote on a sticky note, a small plant for fresh air, or an image representing your dream outcome. These visual anchors keep your objectives top of mind and spark positive emotions.
- <u>Eliminate digital distractions</u> – close unused browser tabs, disable non-urgent notifications, and use full-screen focus modes. A minimalist digital environment mirrors your physical space, reducing cognitive load and resisting procrastination.
- <u>Keep necessary tools visible </u>– place your notebook, pens, water, sticky notes, headphones, and any other item needed to perform your best close by with easy access.
- <u>Optimize ergonomics and lighting </u>– a comfortable chair, good lighting, and proper keyboard and screen height make you more comfortable to work on your goals.

- <u>Set clear boundaries with others</u> – talk to coworkers, roommates, family, and friends about your focus time. Let them know if you close your door or have headphones on while working, that you would like to not be disturbed.
- <u>Limit decision burnout</u> – pre-plan your meals for the week, your outfits, and activities to get a head start on not only your day, but your week.

Embrace Progress Over Perfection

Lastly, if I had one piece of great advice to share with you, I would say, "Embrace progress and consistency over perfection." Perfectionism is the enemy of consistency. Living a life of perfection keeps your dreams from coming true because you will be in a constant state of thinking, "it's not ready, I'm not ready, I just need a little more time". Waiting until conditions are perfect or outcomes are flawless will keep you stuck. Instead of wanting everything to be perfect, embrace progress. Show up imperfectly but persistently. Every step forward—no matter how small or messy—is a victory. Consistency isn't about being flawless; it's about being faithful. When you give yourself permission to grow gradually, you unlock the freedom to stay committed long-term.

> I MOVE FORWARD WITH CLARITY, COURAGE, AND CONSISTENCY. EVERY STEP I TAKE BRINGS ME CLOSER TO CRUSHING MY GOALS.
>
> DR. ALBERTA BROWN GREEN

Chapter Seven

Crush Your Goals

"Your goals don't need perfect timing— just a spark. One small step today can set the whole fire in motion.".

- *Dr. ABG*

Here is your wakeup call: your goals aren't waiting on all of the stars to align in your favor—they're waiting on you. Not the polished, over-prepared perfect version of you, but the real you. The one who's tired of spinning in circles, overthinking every single move, and waiting for the perfect moment to change careers, go back to school, write your book, find a new job, or finally stop eating food that isn't good for you and start your health journey.

This chapter is your permission to stop stalling and start showing up for yourself. You don't need more time, more talent, or more tools—all you need is a strategy that works with your talents and strengths, not against them. Crushing your goals isn't just about motivation; it's about method. You need tools that work in real life, not just on paper. Also, crushing your goals isn't about the latest fads or tricks of the trade. It's about clarity, consistency, and the courage to keep moving forward and believe that you can create a strategy, and love the current version of yourself through the process of becoming a new, wiser, and better version.

Goal crushing in action

Big goals don't require locking yourself away in your home or work office for weeks at a time. I actually believed this once upon a time and locked myself away for weeks at a time while completing my dissertation. Trust me when I say that process was not good for my wellbeing or mental health. Crushing your goals requires small, intentional shifts that move you to completion over time. Ready to remove your robe of procrastination and become a finisher?

Let's cover four of my favorite tried-and-true rules that will change the way you approach your day, your mindset, and your momentum.

The 100 Hour Rule teaches you to invest in your talents, not your weaknesses. The 10-10-10 Rule gives you perspective when panic tries to take the wheel. The 5 AM/20-20-20 Rule carves out a sacred hour to fuel your body, mind, and mission. And the 7-Minute Rule? It's your antidote to procrastination—because seven minutes of action beats seven hours of avoidance. These are simple hacks that will shape your future habits and give you the new identity of a GOAL CRUSHER.

The 100 Hour Rule

The 100 Hour Rule reminds us that time is like money, and where you spend it determines your return on investment, and when you spend it, it's gone. Give the biggest chunk of your time to your gifts and talents – meaning what you are GREAT at doing. And sit back and watch how you grow, flourish, and come to life.

If you had 100 free hours to invest in yourself, how would you spend them? Most of us waste too much time trying to fix what we're bad at, instead of sharpening what we're already good at – meaning we underuse and don't give time to our strengths. For instance, you're on the struggle bus, trying your best to function at a company that requires you to sit at a desk for eight hours and create presentations and programs. However, you're naturally gifted in communication. Case in point, why spend 50 hours trying to become a programming genius when you could spend those same hours becoming a world-class communicator? Now, that doesn't mean you ignore your weaknesses completely. If you're "bad" at something essential—like managing money or showing up on time—you can't just shrug and say, "Well, that's not my thing."

But you don't need to pour the majority of your hours into it either. A little focused effort can bring you from "bad" to "functional," and that's enough. Remember, with weaknesses, you don't have to build a palace – you just need a bridge. Consider progress, not perfection.

The sweet spot and biggest opportunity is in your "average" skills. With a little love and practice, average skills can become strong assets. Maybe you're an ok writer or presenter, but with 20 or 30 hours of focused effort and practice on writing, presenting, and organizing, you can become confident, capable, and show up differently. That's the beauty of the 100 Hour Rule: it forces you to be intentional about where you spend your time and how you grow your skills.

Your strongest skills deserve the most hours because they open doors to everything you could imagine in your work and home life. When you give time where you naturally flourish and shine, you gain momentum, energy, and courage, which shrinks obstacles.

So, ask yourself: if you had 100 hours, how many would you give to your strengths, your average skills, and your weaknesses? The answer will tell you a lot about your priorities—and whether you're building on a foundation of strength or wasting time patching cracks that don't matter.

Crush Your Goals With The 100 Hour Rule

Map out your 100 hours: Give 65 hours to your talents and strengths, 20 hours to your average skills, and 10 hours to critical weaknesses.

Pick three skills: One skill you're great at and can master, one you're good at and can improve, and one that is weak but you need to stabilize it. Place short, regular sessions on your calendar that involve investing in your great and good skills as well as managing the weak skills.

What are your thoughts about the 100 Hour Rule, and how will you use this rule with your goal planning?

Reflections: _____

_____

_____

_____

_____

_____

_____

_____

The 10-10-10 Rule

When you're stressing over a goal, pause and ask: how will this matter in 10 minutes, 10 months, and 10 years? Most of the things that keep us awake at night won't even cross our minds a year from now. That missed deadline, awkward conversation, misspelled words in an email or small setback? In 10 minutes, you'll still feel it. In 10 years, you'll laugh about it.

This rule is saturated in perspective. Perspective is a superpower that turns panic into priorities. For instance, most embarrassing situations are short-lived. The 10-10-10 rule teaches you how to put problems in their place. It's like zooming out on a map—you realize that what felt like a mountain is really just a bump in the road. The 10-10-10 Rule also helps you separate the temporary from the timeless or the urgent from the important.

Of course, some decisions and choices do matter long-term. For instance, long-term decisions deserve a large vision. Building healthy habits, investing in finances, relationships, your education, and integrity—those are 10-year decisions that require careful attention. When deciding what's worth stressing over, ask, "Will this choice build or borrow from my future"? Stress less about the things that fade, and focus more on the choices that shape your future. In other words, "don't sweat the small stuff".

When using the 10-10-10, you're not ignoring your feelings—you're giving them context. When you zoom out and look at the bigger picture, you think clearly, breathe easier, and make wiser choices. The noise in your head gets quieter, and your peace overtakes the situation, placing you in the position of power. However, when there is no order or process, the noise in your head can get louder, and panic will creep in, and overtake the situation.

So next time you're spiraling, ask yourself: will this matter in 10 minutes, 10 months, or 10 years? If the answer is "no," let it go. If the answer is "yes," then give it the energy it deserves. Either way, you win—because you're no longer letting stress run the show.

Crush Your Goals With The 10-10-10 Rule

Take up to three sticky notes and write "10-10-10" on each of them. Place them in areas where you perform a lot of work and thinking. If you are about to spiral out of control, look at the sticky and answer the 10 minutes, 10 months, or 10-year questions: If it matters long-term (ten months/minutes) make time and schedule a small action now. If it doesn't, let it go and move on.

What are your thoughts about the 10-10-10 Rule, and how will you use this rule with your goal planning?

Reflections:

_____
_____
_____
_____
_____
_____
_____

The 5 AM/20-20-20 Rule

There's something magical about waking up before the world does. The 5 AM Rule isn't about punishing yourself with early mornings—it's about protecting an hour in your day, giving yourself a head start. We will call this hour the "Power Hour". During this designated hour, move your body for 20 minutes, learn something new for 20 minutes, and write out and organize your tasks for 20 minutes. That's one hour that sets the tone for your entire day.

Movement causes your body to wake up and consume energy. It doesn't require you to move as if you have five days to lose 15 pounds before your 10-year class reunion—stretching, walking, singing in the shower, or dancing around your room counts. Remember, consistency always beats intensity. The point is to tell your body, "We're awake, we're alive, we're ready." Once you tell your body this, the brain will follow.

Learning something that interests you or something needed to enhance your work skills for 20 minutes feeds your mind. Imagine feeding your mind before your job, family, or the world starts asking for bites of it. Read a chapter in a book, listen to motivational or educational podcasts, or study a skill. Imagine how much smarter you'll be after 365 days of 20-minute learning sessions. Just think about it….that's over 120 hours of growth in a year—just from mornings.

Planning guides direction. When your mind is cluttered and your day is noisy, planning keeps you grounded. Think of it as inputting a location in your GPS: you know where you are going before getting on the highway of life. Spend 20 minutes writing out your tasks and goals give your day order. Instead of reacting to life, you're leading it by commanding the process of your day. The 5 AM Rule is less about the clock and more about the commitment. Even if your "5 AM" is 4 AM, 6 AM, or 7 AM, the principle is the same: start your day with movement, learning, and intention.

Crush Your Goals With The 5 AM/20-20-20 Rule

Prepare the night before. Lay out your clothes, pack your workbag, fill your water bottle, and place it with your work bag, bookbag, or purse. Choose a 20-minute workout, choose what you'll read or listen to, and plan your day. Set an alarm away from your nightstand so that you must physically get out of the bed to turn it off. For your checklist, use a sticky or blank sheet of paper, draw three small boxes, and place one word next to each box—move, learn, plan—and check them off after you complete each 20-minute activity. PROTECT YOUR POWER HOUR: turn off all phone notifications, close all computer browsers that don't relate to your power hour, and share with your family, friends or roommate that you won't be able to respond to their needs during this time.

What are your thoughts about the 5 AM/20-20-20 Rule, and how will you use this rule with your goal planning?

*Reflections:*_____

_____

_____

_____

_____

_____

The 7 Minute Rule

Procrastination is sneaky—it convinces you that a task is too big, so you don't even start. The 7 Minute Rule destroys that excuse. Tell yourself, "I can do anything for seven minutes." Write for seven minutes. Clean for seven minutes. Study for seven minutes. Most likely, once you start, you'll keep going past seven minutes.

When I absolutely must focus on a project, email, or something important, I set a seven-minute timer. If the timer goes off and I am not finished, I restart the timer. The beauty of this rule is that it lowers your stress level and allows you to cross the barrier to entry. You don't need to climb the whole mountain—you just need to climb for seven minutes. And often, those first seven minutes are enough to build momentum and often, move you in the direction of pushing through the next seven to ten or even 30 minutes.

Seven minutes shape identity. Each day you act—however small—you're casting a vote for the person you're becoming. "I am someone who shows up, at least for seven minutes." That matters more than a perfect session once a week. Seven minutes also calms fear and courage grows with repetition.

Big goals or large tasks can feel heavy because of the time requirement and commitment. Shrink the goal by giving yourself a small window of time. Even if you stop and breathe at the seven-minute mark, you've still won. You've proven to yourself that you can start. And starting is the hardest part. Seven minutes today leads to twenty minutes tomorrow, and before you know it, you've built a habit.

So, the next time you're staring at a task you don't want to do, don't promise yourself an hour. Promise yourself seven minutes. You'll be amazed at how far seven minutes can take you.

Crush Your Goals With The Seven Minute Rule

Create a seven-minute "first touch" every day. Open the document, write one sentence, practice one chord, send one message, make one phone call. Tiny daily touches keep your goal alive and growing. Define the tiniest "seven-minute first move" for each of your goals. That could be giving yourself seven minutes to try out a new breathing exercise, seven minutes to put together an outfit, seven minutes to work on an email that needs major attention, or seven minutes of yoga. Practice this rule every day—seven minutes of your undivided attention on a work project. Seven minutes of undivided attention to studying. A seven minute phone call with a loved one you've been promising to reach out to for over three weeks. Seven minutes, no drama. Track your streak with a simple tally: "I showed up." If your seven minutes have been productive, stretch the process to ten minutes to complete the task, and decrease it by two minutes if you are working on completing a task faster, but seven minutes is the win.

     Keep a menu of tiny steps ready so you're never stuck figuring out where to begin. When motivation is low, your menu saves the day. Always remember….small steps, big heart, and steady progress will bring you closer to the finish line every single time.

What are your thoughts about the Seven Minute Rule, and how will you use this rule with your goal planning?

*Reflections:*_____

_____

_____

_____

_____

_____

Goal crushing practice

You don't have to wait for the perfect moment to begin crushing your goals—your moment is now. Goals aren't crushed in one giant leap; they're conquered through steady, intentional steps, no matter how small. Allow small actions to replace hesitation. Every time you choose action over hesitation, you are demonstrating to yourself that you are capable, worthy, and destined for success.

Don't underestimate the power of your own amazing momentum— it's your secret weapon: each choice to act builds confidence, proves your capability, and makes the next step easier. Consistency, not a single dramatic effort, is how goals are conquered because the more you try and the more you practice, you become more consistent, which leads to moving forward and becoming unstoppable.

Let's meet Brian, see how his new year is going, listen to the resolutions that he is considering, and see where he's stuck. After reading Brian's story with an eye for which strategies from this book would help him, answer the reflection questions to translate the ideas into a clear plan to crush his goals. Lastly, consider yourself or someone you know. If your story or their story is similar to Brian's, how would you use the strategies to help yourself or a friend?

Brian's Story

Brian, a full-of-life, charismatic young man, is about to find out that he has Type II Diabetes. Brian had completed bloodwork last week and was called by his doctor's office to review his bloodwork, as the doctor was concerned with his test results. As he sat in the doctor's office, waiting on his test results, he submerged himself in numerous TikTok videos to keep his mind from racing through the what-ifs. Brian just celebrated his 23rd birthday a few weeks ago, and whew…. A time was had by all. The drinking, eating, and smoking were a little overboard, but Brian figured what could it hurt – this is how most 23-year-olds celebrate, right?

Brian heard footsteps approaching the door. He quickly tried to turn down the volume on the phone, but he accidentally turned it up. Needless to say, Brian was viewing a not-so-appropriate TikTok for the ears of the elderly.

As he wiggled and sank in his seat from embarrassment, trying his best to turn off the phone, Dr. Norman slightly frowned and sarcastically said, "Sorry to interrupt you, Brian, take your time. I only have seven more patients waiting to see me. After turning his phone to silent mode, Brian sat up in his seat with a nervous smile, mumbling the words, "Hi, Dr. Norman". Hello Brian, glad you were able to come in.

Let's cut straight to the point. Brian, you have Type II diabetes, and your numbers are pretty high. Three years ago, when we discovered that you were pre-diabetic, we discussed managing your weight by diet and exercise as well as taking it easy on your alcohol consumption. Now that you are diabetic, it is time for you to think about your health and your future.

Brian has been fairly active his whole life. He played tee-ball, baseball, football, and soccer in middle and high school. Type II Diabetes is a part of his family history, but he never thought he would ever have to deal with it. You see, Brian has always been on the heavier side of the scale since he was a little boy. He was the kid who would "clean his plate" by eating every single morsel to show his mom that he loved her. It also helped that he thought she was the best cook on the planet.

Brian never worried about getting Type II Diabetes because he naturally thought he was too young… also, he carried his weight well and assumed you had to be morbidly obese to catch it, right?

Before being diagnosed with Type II Diabetes, Brian had many physical signs that he didn't think were too big of a deal. Brian would always find himself sweating for no reason and constantly having to go to the restroom, even if he didn't have a lot of water to drink.

While eating, Brian would feel light-headed and dizzy, followed by needing a nap. A few times, his tiredness would catch up with him. One time, he decided to take a nap in his car after eating a double cheeseburger, biggie fries, and Coke. Needless to say, Brian became dizzy and sleepy and slept right through his lunch break.

After hearing Dr. Norman say the actual words "you have Type II Diabetes", it finally clicked in Brian's mind that it was time to do something about his health. Brian comes from a long line of diabetics and even has an aunt who has lost a leg to the disease and an uncle who passed from diabetes at the age of 50 due to not managing his health appropriately. "Today is the day that I will plan to work on my health," said Brian.

Next month is the start of the New Year, but today is the day that I commit to the resolution of eating clean, exercising, and managing my alcohol consumption.

Reflection Questions

Do you or someone you know relate to Brian's story? If so, what are your thoughts about his story?

_____
_____
_____
_____

What strategies in this book could assist Brian in achieving his goal of working on his health?

Who could be a part of Brian's circle to move him forward toward positive progress, and who might be holding me back?

How can Brian celebrate small wins in a way that feels meaningful to him?

What resistance or distractions have you noticed in Brian's story that can hold him back, and how can he push past them with persistence?

___

Affirmation

"I move forward with clarity, courage, and consistency. Every step I take brings me closer to crushing my goals."

Reflections:___

HEALING YOUR WAY TO THE FINISH LINE REQUIRES YOUR MIND, BODY, AND SPIRIT TO WORK TOGETHER HOLISTICALLY FOR YOUR GOOD.

DR. ALBERTA BROWN GREEN

Chapter Eight

Finding Your Way Forward: Mental Wellness and the Power to Finish Strong

"Clarity of mind is the fuel for completion. When your mental wellness is in check, you unlock the strength to finish what once felt impossible."
– Dr. ABG

Finding Your Way Forward

She sat across from me, eyes heavy with a fatigue that seemed older than just a sleepless night. Her hands twisted and untwisted the Kleenex that held her tears from an issue that had consumed her for an extended amount of time…the issue of how to move forward. Through deep breaths and tears, she whispered, "My mind won't stop racing from the guilt of not being able to do what I know I need to do. I want to set goals, I want to be a better employee, I want to show up for my children, my husband, and for myself, but I can't even focus long enough to do anything or even figure out where to start."

Her voice carried both frustration and exhaustion, the kind that comes from fighting struggles no one else can see. It was clear she'd been running on empty for far too long.

She leaned her head backwards, took a deep breath, and her shoulders dropped as if each exhale drained any ounce of energy she had. She looked down at the empty notebook given to her before the start of our session, as if it were too heavy to pick up.

I leaned forward, my heart aching for her, imagining how lonely and frustrating the hours of her life must feel when every second stretches into an endless loop of worry. In that moment, she wasn't just a struggling parent or a weary professional; she was any one of us who's ever been frozen by fear, trembling over opportunity, or longing for a foothold. And in her silence, I heard the unspoken and desperate plea of every person too afraid to begin.

Her story may feel painfully familiar because so many of us have stood in that heavy, stalled place—uncertain of goals, overwhelmed by racing thoughts, and exhausted by the relentless noise of worry. You are not broken; you are human, carrying weight that needs tending to and a plan that needs direction.

This chapter is about understanding the connection between mental wellness, why it matters in goal-setting, and the power to finish strong – it hands you practical ways to loosen anxiety's grip and turn the ache of starting into action—one small, courageous step that proves you are capable of more than you can ever imagine.

Why Mental Wellness Matters in Goal-Setting

We often underestimate the power of our mental wellness when it comes to finishing goals. Mental wellness shapes the very soil where goals either take root or die. When your mind is calm, clear, and nourished, priorities stay visible and momentum follows naturally; when it's strained, even the best plans feel heavy and distant. For instance, you can have the best organized planner, the boldest vision board, and the most inspiring and moving quotes taped to your wall—but if your mental health is suffering, it's like trying to drive a car, knowing you are on empty…. You won't get far, no matter how many times you crank the car and press the gas.

Have you ever experienced a time when you felt hopeless? Better yet, have you ever sensed that something deeper than fatigue, overwhelm, or stress was happening inside you? If so, take a minute to write down what you're feeling and any thoughts or patterns that come to mind.

Reflections:

_____

_____

_____

_____

_____

Mental wellness changes how you choose to pursue your goals. A clear, rested mind helps you break big aims into attainable steps, tolerate short-term discomfort, and keep moving forward when progress slows. Anxiety, burnout, or constant low mood corrupts time, magnifies setbacks, and pushes you toward avoiding your goals; when you protect your mental health, you make smarter choices about what to aim for and how to get there, turning ambition into steady, sustainable action.

The young lady, mentioned earlier, did the best thing she could have possibly done for her mental health – she asked for help. Prior to her seeking help, her life was being interrupted by plans being repeatedly postponed, her inability to focus on or resolve small problems, and her self-criticism was at an all-time high. Those signs piled up into exhaustion and paralysis until she finally did the bravest thing—she asked for help.

Speaking with a therapist helped her sort through her thoughts and gave her immediate relief and practical skills: she learned to slow a racing mind, notice where her energy was leaking, and permit herself to rest without guilt. Those sessions didn't erase the hard parts, but they created the mental room she needed to breathe, to turn scattered intentions into concrete steps, and to begin putting her goals on paper with clarity and steady momentum. In other words, the sessions became her

her foundation and safe place to give herself grace.

Choosing the Right Support

Let's pause: seeking help is not weakness — seeking help is wisdom. You wouldn't hesitate to call a mechanic when your car fails or a plumber when a pipe bursts; the same clear logic applies to your mental wellness. When you reach out for support, you're choosing YOU and preventing prolonged struggle, grief, and the failure to start. Choosing YOU accelerates your ability to set, pursue, and finish meaningful goals.

I'll be honest—I've been there too. There was a time when everything felt disjointed, overwhelming, and undoable. I carried the heavy responsibilities of marriage, motherhood, and being a star employee, all while keeping up appearances. This lifestyle pushed me straight into burnout. My mind was cluttered with endless to-dos and a perfectionist voice so loud I could barely think. Saying out loud, "I can't keep doing this the way I've been doing it," and sitting in that chair changed my life.

Therapy gave me practical tools that actually worked. I learned breathing techniques to quiet the noise, grounding exercises to bring me back to the present, and simple ways to break overwhelming tasks into pieces I could manage. Those sessions didn't fix everything overnight, but they created breathable space in my head, gave me routines that supported focus, and reminded me I wasn't broken—I was human.

Therapy dives into underlying concerns, fears, and challenges, and helps you move forward in life by uncovering and healing past wounds or trauma. Life coaching guides your strategy, holds you accountable, and pushes you, through encouragement, to the finish line. Finding the right therapist or life coach is part of your strategy for success, and investing in this relationship is investing in your future victories. Don't let the titles intimidate you. What matters is finding someone who listens without judgment, offers practical tools, and cheers you on when progress feels small. Not every match will feel perfect, and that is okay.

Treat the search like hiring a positive, motivational, and wise friend whose values align with yours, who listens without judgment, and who will serve in the capacity of an accountability partner, even during challenging times.

When you find a therapist or life coach you trust, the work becomes less about surviving and more about building—building clarity, routines, and mental space for action. Therapy or life coaching gives you tools to steady a racing mind, reclaim leaking energy, and grant yourself permission to rest without guilt. Those changes create the breathing room you need to translate intention into small, steady steps and to keep moving toward the life you desire.

Therapy and Human Connection

If you're wondering about therapy or life coaching, hear me out: it's practical help that can be used daily, not just as a last resort. Imagine sitting with someone who hands you a lifeline that can be used immediately—a breathing technique, a way to slow a racing thought, or a plan to chop a big task into a five-minute starter. That one tool can possibly change the next seven minutes, hour, or your whole life. Try one session and treat it like a first date; yes, you will feel anxious, uncomfortable, and nervous, however, be excited about the possibilities of a new you and a new normal. If your first session goes well, great, and if not – meaning you are uncomfortable with the therapist or coach, keep looking until you find someone who is a good fit.

Don't underestimate the power of human connection. You don't have to figure life out alone. Build a circle of support consisting of people who want the best for you—one friend who listens, one accountability partner, one professional—and let them do some of the heavy lifting with you. Sometimes, the best encouragement comes from a simple, "I believe in you", spoken at the right time. If reaching out feels scary, start with a simple step: ask a friend for a recommendation, read one therapist's page, or book a single exploratory session.

Do that for yourself today; you deserve clarity, and that first step will make finishing strong feel possible.

The Power to Finish Strong

Hitting a brick wall, when you're doing the best that you can to complete goals or reach your dreams, feels like trying to sprint through molasses—frustrating, exhausting, and a little messy and embarrassing. But here's the truth: almost everyone stalls at some point, no matter how motivated they started. Acknowledging the struggle without shame is the first step, and recognizing that you need a little help is the second courageous step toward moving forward.

Crushing your goals takes practical skills, processes, and steady perseverance. Use every ally you can find—your boss, a coach, your community, licensed professionals, and a higher power—to rebuild momentum. When you blend strategy, support, and self-care, you don't just cross the finish line; you do it with resilience, confidence, and the help you deserve.

Challenges on the Job? First, consider talking to your boss or mentor about revisiting your goals. Schedule a quick one-on-one, share where you're stuck, and ask if they can help you reshape your objectives. Chances are they've navigated similar challenges themselves and can offer a fresh perspective—or even tweak deadlines and priorities so you can breathe again.

Go into that conversation prepared. Jot down which tasks feel overwhelming, which skills you'd like to strengthen, and any roadblocks that keep popping up and keeping you from being great. Frame it as a team effort: "I want to crush these goals, and I could use your insight on how to realign my plan." A little clarity from above can transform confusion into focus—and remind you that you're not climbing this mountain solo. If workplace guidance still isn't enough, seek a career counselor or life coach—ideally someone with a mental-health background. These professionals specialize in untangling goal-related stress from deeper emotional patterns. They'll help you identify and gently rewire self-sabotaging habits, anxiety loops, and mindset blocks that keep tripping you up.

Lastly, spiritual wellbeing is a must. Treat it as a nonnegotiable in your life's journey. Tap into something bigger than yourself. Whether that's increasing your faith, becoming involved in community service, or a creative outlet, connecting to a larger purpose reframes your personal and professional struggles. A mantra I personally use for spiritual wellbeing is "Lord, give me clarity for the path ahead, strength to complete the work, and humility for the process. Amen.

When your goals serve more than just your own agenda, you gain a momentum of strength that's beyond willpower. Suddenly, your efforts ripple outward—you're not just finishing strong for yourself, but for everyone you inspire.

That "something bigger" can be as simple as volunteering at a local shelter, joining a spiritual study group, or leading a book club. Each act reminds you that progress isn't measured solely by checkboxes on a to-do list. You are part of a grander story, and every step forward—no matter how small—fuels the collective journey.

Still having challenges moving forward?

If you've tried talking to your boss, coaching, mindset shifts, tapping into something bigger, and community connections, yet still feel stuck – I encourage you to seek professional mental health support. Persistent inability to move forward often signals a bigger problem. You could be experiencing anxiety, depression, or burnout. A licensed therapist or psychiatrist can offer diagnoses, coping strategies, or medication support that no number of to-dos can replace.

Know the signs of when to seek the help of a therapist or psychiatrist: if you're chronically plagued with sadness, anxiety, or panic for several weeks, and it interferes with your ability to sleep, eat, work, or maintain healthy relationships, your brain chemistry might need extra help. Furthermore, seek help immediately if you have thoughts of hurting yourself, others, or thoughts of suicide. Reaching out for therapy isn't admitting defeat—it's equipping yourself with every tool available to cross your finish line. Imagine it as calling in reinforcements so you can lead your own life again.

Lastly, allow this chapter to give you permission to say yes to support, therapy, and the strategy to crush the goals that are patiently waiting for you! My friend, you don't have to suffer in silence. You don't have to constantly pretend that everything is ok while your mind is running on overdrive. You can ask for support. You can get help. You can still crush your goals, one clear, intentional step at a time. ask yourself: Am I truly lacking discipline, or am I carrying mental weight that makes it nearly impossible to move forward? Sometimes it's not about laziness, it's about exhaustion, a chemical imbalance, or needing bloodwork done to rule out situations that can be causing the exhaustion. And exhaustion requires not only mental healing, but physical healing as well.

I'll leave you with a promise: I promise, when you care for your mind, your body, and your spirit, your goals will become less overwhelming and will start being more achievable. You will see the light at the end of the tunnel, and you will become the ultimate goal crusher! And that, my friend, is the real secret to finishing strong. Congratulations on becoming a person who finishes what they start -an Ultimate Goal Crusher!

Now, take some time to answer the questions at the end of this chapter, and use the chapter reflection pages for deeper reflection regarding each chapter.

Reflection Questions

What's one mental weight you've been carrying that's kept you from moving forward on your goals?

_____
_____
_____
_____
_____
_____
_____
_____

Who could you reach out to for support—whether a therapist, mentor, or trusted friend? If you don't have names, I encourage you to do your research and find a person for each category.

_____
_____
_____
_____
_____
_____
_____

What's one coping strategy (journaling, exercise, prayer, rest) you could begin practicing this week?

_____

_____

_____

_____

_____

_____

_____

How would your goals change if your mind was clearer and you had more peace and order in your career and life? What would you accomplish?

_____

_____

_____

_____

_____

_____

_____

_____

What are three steps you can take this week to honor your mental health while working toward your goals?

What is your favorite quote, saying, or scripture you will write down to encourage you when you want to quit? If you don't have one, I recommend finding one and writing it in the space below.

Chapter One Reflections:

Chapter Two Reflections:

Chapter Three Reflections:

Chapter Four Reflections:

Chapter Five Reflections:

Chapter Six Reflections:

Chapter Seven Reflections:

Chapter Eight Reflections:

About ABG Professional Development Solutions Services! Give us a call or check out our website – www.abgpds.com

Professional Development Solutions

Our Professional Training and Development Services include but are not limited to: Team and leadership development training, Individual and/or group training, and Professional development workshops and training.

Our Executive Career and Life Coaching focuses on the individual, with services such as career and executive career professional development, life coaching, as well as high school and college professional development.

Mental Health Counseling

ABG Counseling and Career Consulting is well known for providing a caring and trusting counseling relationship experience for their clients through a holistic approach to counseling. The therapists are responsible for providing a safe, non-judgmental environment where you, the client, can explore and identify challenges, problematic areas, and areas of opportunities for growth, renewal, and change.

ABG Counseling and Career Consulting also provides *Executive Career Professional Development, Career Professional Development, Life Coaching for a Better You,* and *High School/College Student Professional Development*

About Us

Our Services
- Professional Trainings
- Management Programs
- Career & Life Coaching
- Mental Health Counseling
- Speaking Engagements

ABG Specialty Trainings
- ABG Win With Strengths
- ABG True Colors Self-Discovery
- ABG Working With Difficult People
- ABG Spoken and Unspoken RULES of Workplace Etiquette
- ABG Half Year Plan
- ABG Inclusion with Diplomacy and Tact
- ABG Empathy: A Gamechanger for the Ever-Changing World of Work, Culture, and Life
- ABG Strategies to De-stress and Recharge your Life After Burnout and Anxiety Online Training

Leadership Development Programs
- ABG Coaching Managers for Success Program
- ABG Leadership Development Program
- ABG Journey to Adulthood Program
- ABG Company-wide Programs

ABG Professional Training & Development Services
- Individual or Group Leadership Training Sessions
- Professional Development Workshops and Training
- Team and Leadership Development Training

Scan for Our Website

Where to find us

 401 Bayou Drive Monroe, LA 71203
 abgpds.com
 info@abgpds.com
 abgpds
 318-801-6584
ABG Professional Development Solutions

Made in the USA
Coppell, TX
24 February 2026